REACHING YOUR CHILD'S HEART

"The book you have in your hands is a combination of biblical wisdom and genuine humility cultivated by years of trial and error learning to parent under God's hand. I love that the book begins by reminding you to pray and ends by emphasizing the need to trust in the Lord with all your heart rather than relying on your own understanding of your child's heart. Read this book and put it to work!"

Miguel Núñez, Professor of Pastoral Leadership, The Southern Baptist Theological Seminary; senior pastor, International Baptist Church of Santo Domingo; president, Wisdom and Integrity Ministries

"Juan and Jeanine outline a biblical and theological framework of practical, gospel-oriented principles for parenting. Each chapter is followed by helpful discussion questions, giving an interactive opportunity for parents to assess and apply these biblical principles in their own families. We highly recommend *Reaching Your Child's Heart* as a very accessible, practical, biblically sound framework for parenting."

David and Sally Michael, Executive Director, Truth78; author; director of publishing and training; Truth78

"I first heard Juan and Jeanine talk about these parenting principles when I was a member at High Pointe Baptist, where Juan serves as senior pastor. Both my wife and I were tremendously blessed by the simple way in which they demystified parenting for us, and we still apply their advice with our kids to this day."

Giancarlo Montemayor, Vice President of Global Publishing, Lifeway Christian Resources

"I have had the privilege of watching Juan and Jeanine Sanchez apply godly principles of parenting to their own children, and their gentleness, wisdom, and patience had a profound effect on our family at a key stage in our parenting. Now they have blessed a new generation of parents with that wise and gentle tone in this excellent book! Every chapter is saturated with biblical truth and practical wisdom, mingled with a conversational tone that makes it appealing. I wholeheartedly endorse this book as a rich treasure that I will pass on as my standard recommendation for parents for years to come!"

Andrew M. Davis, Senior Pastor, First Baptist Church, Durham, NC; author

"*Reaching Your Child's Heart* establishes a firm, biblical foundation for godly parenting and provides a wealth of advice on how to live it out. Not formulaic but eminently practical, the book doesn't stir up guilt but gives the hope of the gospel. Full of helpful illustrations, these seasoned parents walk alongside you with good counsel for the various challenges of parenting in the different stages of your children's lives. Read this book and use the insightful questions to discuss with your spouse and other parents in your church. Whether you're a new parent or have teenagers, it will equip you to shepherd your children, pointing them to Christ."

Keri Folmar, Author of *The Good Portion: Scripture for Every Woman* and Delighting in the Word Bible studies; cohost of *Priscilla Talk* podcast

"In reading this book, you will sit with a kind, warm husband and wife who have walked some miles before you and aren't afraid to show you their scars, so you can gain confidence that parenting is not about your gifting, family tree, or children's attributes but is about the grace provided in the gospel."

Aixa de López, Author; speaker

"After establishing a solidly biblical and gospel-centric foundation, Juan and Jeanine masterfully bring principles to practice through personal examples and humble transparency. They consider themselves travelers with you—sinners parenting sinners, all in need of heart transformation. Anyone in the parenting years will find this book to be a helpful resource that leaves the reader full of hope."

Jack and Mary Delk, Parents and grandparents; Jack is the former pastor of counseling at Bethlehem Baptist Church

REACHING YOUR CHILD'S HEART

A PRACTICAL GUIDE TO FAITHFUL PARENTING

Juan and Jeanine Sanchez

New Growth Press
newgrowthpress.com

New Growth Press, Greensboro, NC 27401
newgrowthpress.com

Cover Design: Faceout Books, faceoutstudio.com
Interior Typesetting and eBook: Lisa Parnell, lparnellbooks.com

ISBN: 978-1-64507-318-5 (paperback)
ISBN: 978-1-64507-319-2 (ebook)

Library of Congress Cataloging-in-Publication Data
Names: Sanchez, Juan, 1965– author. | Sanchez, Jeanine, 1969– author.
Title: Reaching your child's heart : a practical guide to faithful parenting / Juan and Jeanine Sanchez.
Description: Greensboro, NC : New Growth Press, [2024]
Identifiers: LCCN 2024001019 (print) | LCCN 2024001020 (ebook) | ISBN 9781645073185 (print) | ISBN 9781645073192 (ebook)
Subjects: LCSH: Parenting—Religious aspects—Christianity.
Classification: LCC BV4526.3 .S258 2024 (print) | LCC BV4526.3 (ebook) | DDC 248.8/45—dc23/eng/20240216
LC record available at https://lccn.loc.gov/2024001019
LC ebook record available at https://lccn.loc.gov/2024001020

Printed in India

31 30 29 28 27 26 25 24 2 3 4 5 6

We would like to dedicate this book to all those who walked the parenting journey before us and provided wise counsel along the way. We are especially grateful for

Gene and Rosemarie Dreyer
Dan and Ann Campbell
Reggie and Ellen Sheffield

We are also grateful for all of our spiritual parents and grandparents at the churches where we've served:

First Baptist Church, Newberry, FL
First Baptist Church, Eastman, GA
Lagrange Baptist Church, Lagrange, KY
Ryker's Ridge Baptist Church, Madison, IN
High Pointe Baptist Church, Austin, TX

Contents

Introduction

Help! I Am a Parent!

Before you had children, you probably had hopes and dreams about how you would parent and how your children would turn out. One thing was certain: you were *not* going to parent like your parents! You weren't going to make the same mistakes they made raising you. Then, it happened. You became a parent. Very quickly, those hopes and dreams began to dissipate. At some point, you may even have questioned having children. You had a plan. You thought you knew what you were going to do. Then the children came, and nothing turned out as you had hoped. It's possible that you are so frustrated, you've cried out to God for help! Maybe not literally, but in your mind. OK, maybe you also literally cried out for help. It's OK. We have too.

Before we get too far, though, let me warn you that this book is not the "expert" book on parenting that will solve all your problems. Sorry! And this book will not be the last book you'll read on parenting. I'm sure it's not the first. So, why this book? Because we've learned that God has already provided the help parents need. As Christians, he has given us Christ and the good news—the message of salvation. Our children aren't perfect. In fact, they're born sinners. They need Christ, just like we need Christ. And our children don't need perfect parents. They need the perfect Savior. That's good news because God has already provided that too, in Jesus! God has also given us his Word as the standard, not just for parenting, but for all of life. He has given us his Spirit, who fills us with grace, empowers our own obedience, and is conforming us to the image of Jesus. And he has given us each other—the church.

One of the things we learned early in our parenting was to ask for help—as often as possible and before things got too bad. That begins with asking God for help. We're talking about prayer! We did a lot of parenting on our knees—praying for salvation, for safety, for wisdom, for godly husbands (we have all girls), for faithful marriages, and for grandchildren. You get the idea. Also, as we looked around, we noticed there were parents who had journeyed ahead of us. Their children were already grown, or, at least, much older than our girls. We marveled as they related with their children, and their children responded well. We wanted to know what they did, how they did it, and why it worked. When I (Juan) served as a youth minister in a rural church in Florida, we became friends with one of our deacons and his family. He and his wife were raising three daughters. At that time, Jeanine and I were just married, so we didn't have children. We spent a lot of time in their home. We watched them parent. We befriended their daughters. It was a joy to watch and learn as a young couple without children.

Then, we started having children of our own. Who knew that, in God's providence, we would raise five daughters?! We had no idea what we were doing. As far as I knew, Jeanine would handle all the baby stuff, and I would focus on completing my undergraduate degree. We knew nothing! We were supposed to attend birthing classes, where they taught some basics of baby care, but our first daughter came early. We only made it to one class. So there we were, a young couple in our twenties. We brought a baby home, and we didn't know what to do. When she cried at night, I would awaken Jeanine and ask her to feed the baby. In fact, whenever she cried, I asked Jeanine to feed her. That's the only way we knew to get her to stop crying.

As our first daughter grew, she moved to a toddler bed. Our bedtime routine was watching Winnie the Pooh videos until she became sleepy. Then I would put her to bed. By her bedside, on my knees, I would pat her back until she fell asleep. I then tried to crawl out of the room on my hands and knees as quietly as possible. If she made a sound or moved, I hurried to her bedside and began patting her back again. She was four years old before she learned to sleep through the night. *Help!* I thought to myself. *Parenting can't be like this forever, right?!* When Jeanine became pregnant again, I told her I'd had enough. We could not go on with another child in the same way. I said, "You need to figure something out because we're not doing it the same way again!" Looking back, I see how selfish I was. *You* figure it out?! Wasn't that *our* job together?

Needless to say, we got help. This was the beginning of our transformation. Well, Jeanine's transformation, to be honest. I was still the same selfish Juan. In fact, for the first six years of our marriage, I assumed Jeanine was supposed to take care of the babies and toddlers. At some point, when they were potty trained, could communicate verbally, and could take care of themselves, I would step in and take over. Sure, I'm using hyperbole, but not by much. For six years I neglected my responsibilities as a parent. And for six years, Jeanine read the parenting books and faithfully prayed that God would awaken me to my responsibilities. Thankfully, God did.

About six years into our marriage, Jeanine asked me to go with her to a parenting conference. I was reluctant, but I knew I needed to support her. Much to my surprise, the Lord gripped me. I tend to think theologically, and, for the first time, a pastor showed me my responsibilities from Scripture. The speaker made a biblical and theological argument for the role of parents in the home and for how we are to raise our children in a manner that glorifies God. That stayed with me. I returned home a changed man. Well, a changed father, at least. I began to take my parental responsibility seriously. I began to lead in instructing and disciplining my children at home. Instead of letting Winnie the Pooh put our daughter to bed, I became more intentional with our bedtime routine. We started reading aloud together. As I look back on that time, I thank God. I also know Jeanine thanks God! By God's grace, he has allowed us to raise five daughters. They are not perfect. Neither are we. In God's mercy, they all profess faith in Christ. As we have sought to shape our daughters to reflect the image of God, the Lord has used them to shape us as well. So, we write this book together, not as experts, but as fellow parents who cried out for help!

What to Expect

We're glad you picked up this book. Think of it as a collection of lessons we've learned along the way and want to pass along to others on this journey called parenting. You may have already learned some of those lessons. That's great! We love learning from those who have walked ahead of us. And I suspect some lessons we've learned will be helpful to you. That's why we've written this book. First, we want to ground our conversation in God's Word. For those, like me, who need to be convinced (or reminded) from Scripture of what we should be doing and aiming at as we parent, we begin in chapter 1 by laying the biblical and theological foundation for parenting. Our desire in parenting should be the same as God's. The problem is that, because of Adam's sin, we are all born sinners. So in chapter 2, we confront the reality of the context of parenting: the fall. We are sinners ourselves, parenting sinners who need a new heart. And we pray we will have the opportunity to parent children who will embrace Christ, though they too will struggle with sin. If we don't realize that, much of our parenting will be nothing more than behavior modification. Having laid down that biblical and theological foundation, we provide a framework for Christian parenting in chapter 3.

We then move on from the biblical and theological foundations of Christian parenting to explain our biblical responsibilities: to engage in spiritual warfare and faith-fueled prayer for our children (chapter 4), to display the gospel through parental example (chapter 5), and to teach the gospel from God's Word (chapter 6). Of course, one of the challenges of parenting is how to discipline our children. So, in chapter 7, we take time to walk through some proverbs to find biblical guidance. Our aim is to ground both our role and our responsibilities as parents in Scripture.

Of course, if you're looking for help right *now*, the questions you want answers to are the "How" questions. That's what we hope to provide in chapters 8–10. We can't say everything in these chapters, nor would we want to. Instead, think of each of these chapters as an hour-long conversation over coffee. In chapter 8, Jeanine and I sit down with parents of younger children (0–5 years) and talk about the most important things parents should know during those years. Again, we won't touch on everything. We pray it's helpful. We continue our "coffee conversations" in chapters 9 (6–12 years) and 10 (13–18 years). Regardless of the age of your children, we encourage you to read all three practical chapters. Parenting is not formulaic, so many of the Bible's principles for parenting are the same throughout the different stages and ages of a child.

At the beginning of each chapter, we've stated the principle we will emphasize throughout that chapter. And at the end of each chapter, we've written some discussion questions to help you continue the conversation with your spouse or with others who will encourage you. Find other parents, read this book together, and spend time encouraging, praying for, and learning from one another. We especially encourage you to include single parents among your conversation partners.

We know some of you will be tempted to go straight to the "how-to" section (chapters 8–10). We can't stop you. It's your book, now that you've bought it. So you can start wherever you want. But we must warn you: going straight to the application chapters may produce some desired immediate results but leave you frustrated in the long run. We want to encourage you to parent with eternity in mind. Think of it this way: have you ever wanted to lose weight? It's easy to lose weight quickly. Lots of diets are designed to help you see immediate results. The problem is those results aren't sustainable. Instead, if you want to lose weight and keep it off, you need to change your thinking and make healthy, sustainable, and lifelong choices. Skipping to the application chapters is like starting a carb-free diet or fasting. You may see immediate results, but it's not sustainable. We encourage you to take it slow. Read the book with your Bible in hand. Write down questions that come to mind. Remember that we are parenting for the long haul, not the moment.

Finally, we remind you to pray—pray for your children, that God would give them new hearts so they may follow after Christ all the days of their lives. And pray for yourself, that the Lord would grant you the grace to learn from his Word, that you may share his heart and begin to desire for your children what God desires—that they may be godly, reflecting his image, for his glory.

To God be the glory!

Juan and Jeanine Sanchez

Chapter 1

God's Desire for Godly Offspring

Principle: Our desire for our children should be the same as God's: that they would be children who reflect God's image and display his glory in all they think, say, and do.

Before Jeanine and I got married, we had the usual premarital conversations. We talked about communication, finances, intimacy, and, of course, having children. I'm more than a little embarrassed to admit that most of those conversations occurred from a place of ignorance, immaturity, pride, and idealism. We were ignorant as to what having children would be like, much less parenting. And being immature and thinking more highly of ourselves than we ought, we were idealistic in just about everything: the number of children we would have, what gender they would be, how we would raise them, how they would turn out. We even had an ideal timeline. We would spend the first five years of marriage getting to know each other before having children. Like I said, we were ignorant, immature, proud, and idealistic.

On June 29, 1990, our wedding day finally arrived. It was all we had hoped for and more. On the advice of a friend, we postponed our honeymoon for six months, so that we might enjoy it without the exhaustion of a wedding weekend. So, at the end of December, we went to New York City to celebrate New Year's Eve in the Big Apple. It was a wonderful experience. Our plan was working perfectly—spend time as a couple getting to know one another, have fun together, and grow in our love for each other. But everything changed after we returned home. I was completing my undergraduate studies before enrolling in seminary when one day, Jeanine met me for lunch on campus and told me that she was pregnant. I was stunned. I didn't know what to say. That was not our plan. But after a few moments, I hugged her awkwardly and said, "Congratulations." It wasn't my best moment, but I didn't know how else to respond. I had arrived on campus that morning a young married adult, and I left a parent. I wasn't ready for that. She wasn't ready for that. No one is ever truly ready to be a parent. Thankfully, the Lord was gracious. As the baby grew in Jeanine's womb, we began to look forward to all that having a child would entail. Jeanine read books about pregnancy and raising children. I thought about names and wondered what gender the baby was. In no time, we were thrilled with the idea of having a child.

Like all expectant parents, we began to think about what we desired for our child's future. We wanted a perfect child and assumed we would be perfect parents. It's not that our desires weren't good. It's that they were too weak. As new or young parents, we tend to settle for temporal desires like a baby with "ten fingers and toes," a child who will be smart or athletic, or a person who will contribute to society. But our greatest desire as a parent should be the same as God's: godly offspring—children who have a new heart and reflect the image and glory of God in all they say, think, and do. Our highest calling as parents, then, is to be God's instruments as he shapes and molds them into the image of Christ. In the words of Paul Tripp, there is "nothing more important in your life than being one of God's tools to form a human soul."[1] So, to understand our role as parents, we want to lay a biblical and theological foundation. Our aim in this chapter is to present a grand vision of biblical parenting that will define the task and encourage you in it. Though it may be surprising to start a parenting book with theology, it is vital to lay that foundation. It is from the foundation of sound doctrine that good practice flows. So let's look at God's desire for godly offspring revealed in creation, our sin and its effects, and God's plan to redeem his people in order to produce godly offspring.

God's Desire Revealed in Creation

When God created Adam and Eve, he blessed them and told them to "be fruitful and multiply, fill the earth, and subdue it" (Genesis 1:28). One reason God brings the man and woman together in marriage is that he seeks godly offspring. In other words, God's intention from the beginning was to have a people who reflected his image. And he brought the man and the woman together as the means through which to produce that people. As Joyce Baldwin notes in her commentary on Malachi 2:15, "God made two human beings one with the specific purpose of giving them *godly offspring*."[2] But God's design for the family is not simply for a man and a woman to marry and populate the earth with children. If it were, then the goal for a husband and wife would be to have as many children as biologically possible. Instead, God desires godly offspring. Another way of saying it is that God wants children who are like him—children who reflect his image and glory.

Though theologians disagree about what it means to be made in God's image, we can, at least, make a couple of preliminary conclusions. Throughout the Old Testament, an *image* is a physical representation of a god. Now, being created in God's image doesn't mean God is a physical being or that he looks like us. After all, God is a Spirit. To be in God's image means we were created as God's physical representatives on earth. Can you imagine? We are created to represent God on the earth as his kings and queens over his creation. The word *likeness* is used in a similar manner to how we would use it today. "Like father, like son. Like mother, like daughter." We were created to be *like* God in certain ways. Clearly, God has unique characteristics or attributes that we do not share, such as independence (aseity), unchangeableness (immutability), and infinity (being without limitation in relation to time and space). Still, God communicates certain attributes to us—love, wisdom, holiness, righteousness, and justice. As those who bear

God's image, godly offspring reflect the character of their Father in heaven and exercise dominion over his creation as his representative rulers.

Our Sin and Its Effects

The creation mandate to be fruitful and multiply and fill the earth and exercise dominion was given in the context of the garden before the fall. Why is that important? Because before the fall, to produce godly offspring all Adam and Eve had to do was have children. But when our first parents rebelled against God, they introduced sin into the creation and passed on to us their sin, guilt, corruption, and condemnation (Romans 5:12). The effects of the fall on us are so radical and profound that we cannot overcome them ourselves. As a result of the fall, our natural inclination is toward sin and selfishness, which naturally leads to interpersonal conflict, the battle for control, the distortion of our roles, and the neglect of our responsibilities (Genesis 3:14–19). As you can imagine, this not only affects our children, but it also affects our parenting. We will unpack the problem of sin in depth in chapter 2. Right now, though, we want to encourage you with the good news that we are not left hopeless in our sin

God's Redemption and Restoration

Isn't it just like God to give us a glimpse of hope, even in the middle of a curse? In Genesis 3:15, even as God reveals that, because of the fall, the children of the woman and the children of the serpent will be in perpetual conflict, God announces that the woman will have a child who will crush the serpent's head.

The promised Savior will come from the line of Abraham. To him, God promises land, descendants, and a great name. And through his promised descendant, the world will be blessed (Genesis 12:1–3). By the end of Genesis, the promise of descendants is fulfilled, but they are not yet in the Promised Land or together as a nation. So in Exodus, God delivers Abraham's descendants from slavery in Egypt and makes them his people. Israel is God's son, and they will be his special people who will represent God's rule on the earth to the surrounding nations (Exodus 19:4–6). Sound familiar? God has not abandoned his plan for his children to represent his rule, reflect his image, and display his glory.

So, to distinguish his people from the surrounding nations, God makes a covenant with them and gives them the Law (Exodus 20–24). The Law outlines how they are to relate to God and to one another as his holy, godly children. If they are to be God's people, they must obey God and keep his covenant (Exodus 19:5). God promises blessings for all who obey him and curses for all who disobey him. And yet, because they are sinful, Israel almost immediately disobeys, making for themselves an idol that is meant to represent who God is. God, though, is merciful and renews his covenant with them (Exodus 34). This will be the ongoing pattern of Israel's sin. God calls them to obedience. They disobey his Law. God calls them to repentance and promises forgiveness. Israel returns to God. Then they disobey again. The problem? They need a new heart (Deuteronomy 10:16).

God knows they will not obey. They cannot obey (Deuteronomy 31:20). But the Law exposes their sin and points them to their need for salvation. Though they eventually reject God and are removed from the place where God promised to live with them, God promises to restore his people on the basis of a new covenant in which all God's people will have new hearts, will have their sins forgiven, and will receive God's Spirit, who will live in them and empower them to obey (Jeremiah 31:31–34; Ezekiel 36:22–27). How can this be?! God the Father sent God the Son to take on our humanity, keep the covenant his people could not keep, and obey the Law they could not obey. By his perfect obedience, Jesus fulfilled the Law. By his sacrificial death, he received the curses for disobeying the Law. By his resurrection, he received vindication from the Father, who accepted his saving work and opened the door to salvation. This promised descendant from Eve defeated the serpent and crushed the serpent's head on the cross. This promised descendant from Abraham's line is now the one through whom all will be saved. Whoever blesses him will be blessed. Whoever curses him will be cursed.

Isn't that just like God?! Because we inherited Adam's sin, he knew we could not obey. So he sent his beloved Son to obey the Law we could not keep and receive the penalty for our disobedience. Now all who believe in Jesus have Jesus's obedience and payment for disobedience accounted to them. The Law exposes and even increases our sin in order to point us to Christ, the One who saves us from sin and empowers us to obey by his Spirit in us. So God is producing godly offspring, not through biological birth, but through the new birth, in which God's children receive new hearts, forgiveness of sins, and the indwelling Spirit. God works by his Spirit and his Word and his church to transform us into the image of his Son (2 Corinthians 3:18).

The Parenting Task

God is producing godly offspring through the proclamation of the gospel and the regenerating work of the Spirit. Our task as parents, then, is to raise our children in a context where they are regularly exposed to the truth of the gospel by our lives and our words. As parents, we pray that the Holy Spirit will use what we've taught our children to draw them to Jesus. We are God's instruments through whom he is reaching their hearts to draw them to his Son. This is the most important job we have. We plant the seed of the gospel. We water it. God gives it life and causes it to grow.

Mom and Dad, these glorious truths of the gospel must first be in our hearts before we can pass them on to our children. All who are in Christ are no longer sinners by nature, but we still battle with sin. As we grow in the grace and knowledge of Christ, we are to let go of old ways of thinking and renew our minds with the gospel. We must constantly battle against our sin, knowing that we are forgiven, justified by grace through faith, and empowered by the Spirit to obey. The process of being conformed to the image of Christ is a lifelong work of God in our lives. We are not perfect, but we are being perfected. And that perfecting work of God in our lives will last our entire lives. Understanding this lifelong work should not only guide and inform our Christian life, but it should also guide and inform our parenting. It should lead us to parent by faith, with patient endurance, knowing only God can save our children, and trusting that he will one day complete the work he has begun in his children (Philippians 1:6).

Dads, let me (Juan) speak to you directly. As a result of the fall, we are prone either to passivity or control. Because of our fears and doubts, we will likely vacillate between the two. Take me, for example. For the first six years of our marriage, I was a passive husband. It wasn't intentional. I was busy with work and ministry and let Jeanine handle things at home until the Lord convicted me. Jeanine was gracious and patient with me, giving me room to fail as I took on more responsibilities at home. At other times, due to my military background, I ran our house like a boot camp. Again, Jeanine was gracious, helping me build relationships with the girls. Brothers, are you leading in your home according to God's design? Have you abdicated your leadership responsibilities, or are you vying for control? Know that our Lord is full of mercy and grace. Bring your sins, failures, and deficiencies to him, and he will forgive you. Then sit down with your wife and ask her for help (do this when you are not in conflict).

Moms, God created you to be your husband's partner—to help him in all things. We do need the help! I've spoken with enough men who, like me, recognized their failures at home and wanted to change, but who have concluded that no matter how hard they tried, it would never be good enough. So help your husband. Be hopeful for him. Build him up. Encourage the good things he does. Help him see his weaknesses. Together, seek an older couple to guide you. Talk to your pastors. You don't have to parent alone.

A word to single parents: whether you find yourself single by choice or by circumstance, you don't have to parent alone either. Because Jesus has established a new covenant by which he is gathering a new family by faith in him, this new everlasting family is not produced biologically (John 1:12–13). In Christ, we are brothers and sisters. And in the church, we have spiritual fathers, mothers, and grandparents. God has given you his Son, his Spirit, his Word, and his people to help you raise your children. So, allow other families in your church to envelop you and your children into their lives. Seek out older, wiser parents you admire. Learn from parents who are a stage or two in front of you. Ask for help from your pastors. Don't go at it alone.

Parenting is hard! It exposes our sins and weaknesses. Thankfully, God is forgiving, and he has made us to complement each other. We all want to be faithful parents. We all want our families to flourish. So, let us encourage you to work together. Bear one another's burdens. Overlook small offenses. Forgive one another. Encourage one another. Be patient with one another. Pray for one another. Love one another. Honor one another. And speak words to one another that build up.

Conclusion

Too often our parenting feels like mere survival. We're just trying to get through the day. But that's not biblical parenting. Our aim in this chapter was to present a grand vision of biblical parenting that would define the task and encourage you in it. Parenting is hard work, but we're not alone. We have Christ. We have the Spirit. We have God's Word. And we have each other.

Our hope is that as you read this book, the Lord may recalibrate your heart and reignite your desire to raise children in the training and instruction of the Lord (Ephesians 6:4). We plant the seeds of God's Word and his gospel in the minds and hearts of our children. We water those seeds through loving instruction and godly example. We pray for God to give the growth. And we rest in Christ to do his work by his grace and his Spirit. Too often our desires for our children are too weak—that they would be productive in society, that they would get a good education, that they would marry well, that they would be successful in a career. These are good desires, but they are not ultimate. After all, what will it profit your child if she gains the whole world but loses her soul? So, let us parent now with the end in view. Let us begin by admitting that parenting is an impossible task when done in our strength and for wrong ends. And let us continue by resting in the God who has given us his Son in order to save us from our sins. If he has not withheld his Son, he will not withhold anything we need to be faithful parents (Romans 8:32).

Talking Together

In each chapter, we will take time at the end to help you have conversations with your spouse. If you are a single parent or working through this alone, share your reflections with a trusted friend or loved one. Invite a trusted friend to be an encourager.

Personal Story—Jeanine: When Juan and I began having these conversations they didn't go as planned. Don't assume you will understand each other and agree as you begin these conversations. Prepare yourself. Pray for grace and humility. Fight to think the best of each other. Ask clarifying questions. Provide concrete examples. Establish ground rules. Be willing to call a "time out" if things get heated. Remember that you are seeking the same goal—to raise children for the glory of God.

What might the marital conversations mentioned earlier look like for you? Sit down during a time where you are not at odds (that's very important!) and ask each other the questions below (allow this conversation to flow into other questions that you need to address):

1. Husband: Ask your wife, "Do you see me as a passive or active leader in our home?" Notice that I'm not hitting just parenting here; it's also about marriage. The stronger your marriage is, the stronger your parenting will be. Be gracious and humble as you listen. Pray for God's grace. Remember that even if she states things in a way that feels hurtful, she is trying to help. Be patient as she may have bottled-up feelings of hurt or discouragement. So, listen.

Feel free to ask clarifying questions, but don't defend yourself. Let her share freely.

2. Wife: Ask your husband, "Do you see me as mainly as your partner and helper, or as your critic?" Likewise, be gracious and humble as you listen. Patiently listen, asking clarifying questions, but don't defend yourself. Let him share freely.
3. At the end of each chapter, we will ask you to make a list of topics you would like to discuss with your spouse, loved one, trusted friend, or study group as a result of your reading. You don't have to tackle every topic in one sitting, and we encourage you to have these conversations outside of times of conflict. With those ground rules in place, make a list of topics you would like to discuss with your spouse.
   a. Husband and Wife: Make a list of the concerns you shared. Pray together, asking the Lord to help you grow in his grace. Keep that list and pray through it regularly. Come back to this list and give thanks to God for whatever progress he grants.
   b. Single Parent: Make a list of areas you would like to grow in. Make a list of people and families in your church that could help you. Identify a trusted friend you may invite to walk with you through this study.
   c. Study Group: Make a list of your children and consider how to pray for them as you work through this study. Make a personal list of areas you want to grow in as you work through this study. Make a point to be open, honest, and vulnerable with your group.

Chapter 2

The Heart of the Problem

Principle: If we are to parent in a way that honors God and does not frustrate our children, we must understand and account for the problem of sin.

Jeanine and I worked hard to train our girls to obey completely and with a submissive heart. That was the Sanchez standard. Imagine my surprise when, as I was onstage speaking at a student conference, in walked Jeanine with our two-year-old daughter who was supposed to be in the camp nursery. As soon as I finished my talk, Jeanine approached me with a serious look on her face. "What's wrong?" I asked. "Well," she said, "our daughter got into trouble in the nursery, and they called me to pick her up."

Clearly, I thought to myself, *the nursery workers didn't hold the two-year-old to our standard. If they had,* I was certain, *they would have managed the situation. She's only a toddler, after all. And besides, children rise to the standard set for them.* So, I marched Jeanine and the guilty two-year-old back to the camp nursery to instruct the workers on what the Sanchezes expect of their children. When we arrived, I found our daughter's nursery workers. Not surprisingly, they were college students who'd never parented. So, with all the confidence in the world in my parental wisdom, I explained our standard. Respectfully, the nursery worker replied, "Yes, Mr. Sanchez. I understand. I've just never seen a child throw furniture before." "WHAT?!" I responded. The nursery worker calmly explained that when coloring time was over, our two-year-old wanted to continue. When the workers asked her to stop and directed her to the next activity, she threw a chair across the room. So much for our standard.

What possessed our two-year-old daughter to respond with such anger? Simply stated, sin. The real issue was not that she sinned when she threw the chair. The real issue is that she was born a sinner. Throughout Scripture, the word *heart* is often used to describe the inner person—the source of our thoughts, feelings, and actions. As Jesus declares, "For from within, out of people's hearts, come evil thoughts, sexual immoralities, thefts, murders, adulteries, greed, evil actions, deceit, self-indulgence, envy, slander, pride, and foolishness. All these evil things come from within and defile a person" (Mark 7:21–23). This is a reality some parents, teachers, and, yes, even nursery workers forget, ignore, or reject. But understanding the sinful human condition is of great importance in parenting because if we assume our children are born good and that they only need right instruction and a good environment, we will raise either frustrated, despondent children or proud, self-righteous ones.

Some children will be frustrated because they won't be able to meet your standard. Time after time, they will miss the mark, face discipline, and continue to fail. That trajectory is likely to lead to despondency. If we don't understand that, because of sin, our children are unable to obey in their own strength, we may crush our children under the weight of rules and commands they are unable to fulfill. Other children, however, flourish under rules-based righteousness. These children become proud in their ability to please their parents and, eventually, become self-righteous in their obedience. And, of course, there are those children who flagrantly disobey. Remember that the parent-pleasing Pharisee is just as guilty as the zealous rebel. Both are in danger of God's judgment. Therefore, both need God's salvation.

As much as we want our children to obey, the problem is that they are born with hard hearts. That doesn't mean we shouldn't expect obedience. Just like the Law in the life of Israel, holding our children to a biblical standard shows them their sin and points them to their need for Christ (Romans 7:7–25). But if we are to be faithful parents, we need to understand how Adam's rebellion against God has affected all of us, not just our children. Sadly, we are all born into this world in union with our father Adam, having inherited his sin, desiring to practice his rebellion, and deserving his judgment. But, thankfully, the story doesn't end there.

Our Inherited Sinful Condition

When our two-year-old threw a chair across the nursery room at the conference center, she was simply acting according to her nature. Listen to how the Bible describes our inherited sinful condition:

> And you were dead in your trespasses and sins in which you previously walked according to the ways of this world, according to the ruler of the power of the air, the spirit now working in the disobedient. We too all previously lived among them in our fleshly desires, carrying out the inclinations of our flesh and thoughts, and we were by nature children under wrath as the others were also. (Ephesians 2:1–3)

Speaking to the Ephesian Christians, Paul describes their former human condition as "dead in your trespasses and sins" (v. 1). The word "trespass" pictures someone taking a wrong step and losing one's footing. It means "a violation of a moral standard." "Sin" is a general word that indicates a departure from a moral standard. It means "wrongdoing." By putting "trespasses and sins" together, Paul encompasses all sin, whether small or large, whether done in ignorance or with willful rebellion. Because of their sin, Paul describes the Ephesian Christians' spiritual condition as "dead" (v. 1). Here we see our relation to Adam. Because we were born united with Adam, we inherited his sin and live under a sentence of death (Genesis 2:16–17). And being spiritually dead, we are unable to respond to God. Think of it this way: you are at a funeral, and a grieving family member walks up to the open casket and begins screaming for their loved one to "get up!" What do you think will happen? Nothing. Dead people don't respond. Dead people can't respond. That's our sinful human condition—"dead in our trespasses and sins" (v. 1).

To be dead in sin, though, is a spiritual condition. It means that we live under the influence of the world, the flesh, and the devil. We see all three of these forces at work in the Ephesians passage above. In our sinful condition, we are worldly, living "according to the ways of this world," reflecting its cares and attitudes rather than God's (Ephesians 2:2). Satan, of course, is "the ruler of this world" (John 12:31). Paul describes him as the "ruler of the power of the air" (Ephesians 2:2). The idea is that Satan is loose, and he works directly to influence people to rebel against God. This is what happened to Adam in the garden. The devil is still at work, blinding unbelievers and leading sinful humanity to reject God's rule and rage against King Jesus (Psalm 2:1–6), for he is "the spirit now working in the disobedient" (Ephesians 2:2). The most common way the devil influences us to sin is through our own sinful desires: "our flesh" (Ephesians 2:3). Through his lies, Satan deceives us and lures us through the very things we wrongfully want (James 1:14–15). As a result, in our unredeemed state, we are "children under wrath" (Ephesians 2:3).

This is the context for our parenting. We must understand we are parenting children who need new hearts; otherwise, we only change behavior. One of the greatest dangers in parenting is the temptation to settle for well-behaved children who don't see a need for Christ's redeeming love. We are parenting children born in sin, and they need to be rescued out of the kingdom of darkness and transferred into the kingdom of God's Son, just as we were (Colossians 1:13–14). Remember that our theology informs and drives our actions, including our parenting. What we believe about God, Christ, sin, and humanity will determine how we parent. And sadly, the doctrine of inherited (original) sin is not popular. It seems that, even among professing Christians, we've bought into the secular idea that our kids are born good, and it is their environment that ruins them. This perspective places an unbearable weight on parents and unreasonable expectations on children. It also offers little hope for children who live in difficult environments. While it is true that our environments shape us, they do not determine who we become. That's why the gospel is good news. That's why Bible stories are so encouraging. Esther was taken from her family as a young woman and forced to marry a pagan king (Esther 2). Daniel, Shadrach, Meshach, and Abednego were stolen from their home as teenagers and made to serve in the court of a foreign king (Daniel 1). Talk about tough environments. Then there's Samson. By all accounts, he was raised by two loving parents in a godly environment (Judges 13), and yet he was characterized by constant rebellion (Judges 14–16). In all cases, though, God worked through these frail, sinful human beings to accomplish his will.

No, our environment doesn't determine us. We are sinful by nature. So don't be surprised by your child's sinful behavior. Before she can even speak, she throws her food in your face. When he doesn't get his way, he falls on the floor in a fit of anger or throws a chair across a room. Then, when they can speak, they boldly lie to your face. How did this happen? Who taught him to throw his body to the ground? Where did they learn to lie? How did she know to bite her brother when he made her angry? Did you teach your children to sin? Of course not! (Although they do copy some of your behaviors, don't they?) They do it naturally, because they, like the rest of us, were born into this world as sons and daughters of Adam, and we have inherited his sin, rebellion, corruption, and condemnation. But there is hope. While all of us are born dead in our sins and, consequently, are children of the devil, in Christ, God rescues us from the domain of darkness and Satan's rule and transfers us "into the kingdom of the Son he loves" (Colossians 1:13).

The Heart, the Law, and the Gospel

So, to be faithful parents, we need to understand the doctrine of inherited sin, and we need to understand the gospel of Jesus Christ.

We need to remember that our children are sinners by nature, but the gospel offers hope to all rebels. And we need to remember that, even with a new heart and God's Spirit, we and our children will still struggle with sin. So keep in mind that your children are sinners by nature, and that until they are saved and have the Holy Spirit at work inside them, they are not empowered to obey as we are.

How, then, shall we parent children who are sinners by nature? Let's begin by considering the role of the Law in the life of Israel. Why? Because, like our children, God describes Israel as having a heart of stone. Israel needed a (new, circumcised) heart of flesh and God's indwelling Spirit (Ezekiel 36:26–27). Still, God gave them the Law and expected whole-hearted obedience. As we said in chapter 1, God knew they could not obey, but he demanded obedience in order to expose their sin and point them to the only one who could obey, namely, Jesus.

God also provided priests to teach his Word, leaders (elders, judges, kings) to lead them to obey his Word, and prophets to call them back when they disobeyed God's Word. God's Spirit was with these leaders, so that they could lead faithfully in keeping God's covenant. Sadly, Israel's leaders failed them. This too showed their need for a better prophet, priest, and king. Furthermore, on the level of the individual family, God commanded parents to raise their children in the instruction of the Law, so that it was part of their everyday lives (Deuteronomy 6:4–9). Both God's provisions for his people as a whole and his commands for each family are instructive for us as we think about parenting children who are rebellious by nature.

Under the new covenant, we, as God's people, have the Spirit dwelling in us. And in Christ, we are a royal priesthood (1 Peter 2:9). We no longer need a formal priesthood teaching us God's Word because we have direct access to God, through Christ, by his Spirit. So now, we know God personally, and we teach each other by speaking the truth in love. As Spirit-filled Christian parents,

God has called us to shepherd our unbelieving children, teaching them God's Word. Although our children need a new heart that only God can give, we are planting in their hearts and minds the word that is able to save them (James 1:21). We will talk specifically about how to instruct our children in the chapters that follow. For now, know that you are God's shepherd for the children he has given you.

Even though we know our children will be unable to obey us fully, we still maintain a standard of obedience, even from an early age. The fact that they have hard hearts does not free them from that expectation. By expecting obedience, we are positively teaching God's standard. By teaching God's Word, you are both building a biblical framework for their understanding of God and the gospel, on the one hand, and exposing their sinful hearts on the other. As we teach God's Word and discipline for disobedience, we are pointing our children to their real need—Jesus Christ, the one mediator between God and man. He alone can remove hard hearts and replace them with hearts that beat for him. But we need to remember that our children are sinners by nature and be patient with them as our heavenly Father was and continues to be patient with us.

Conclusion

Parenting is hard. Parenting is often frustrating. Too many of our days seem to bear no fruit. If we are to parent faithfully, we must remember that, just like we were, our children are born with hard hearts and in need of a new heart that beats for God. They need God's Spirit to empower them to obey. Only God can give them that. Our task is to teach them God's standard, show them God's patience with sinners, and pray God would save them. And even with believing children, we must continue teaching them God's Word, show them God's patient love, and pray for their holiness. That's the task. How do we do that? That's the focus of our next chapter.

Talking Together

When we forget the doctrine of inherited sin, we will often find ourselves trying to change our children's hearts in our own strength. You might be trying to change your child's heart if you find yourself pleading with them to obey for reasons other than God's glory.

Do you ever find yourself saying things like, "Honey, please clean your room like I've asked for the past ten minutes. I'm just exhausted"? Or, how about "When I was growing up, we would never have thought of behaving that way"? This is a form of manipulation. It may change behavior, but it does not reach the heart. And then there's "Sweetie, Jesus wants you to ask him into your heart so you can go to heaven" when all you really want your child to do is quit acting like the little (or big) sinner that your child is. Remember that we may change their behavior for a brief minute, but only God can change their hearts.

1. What are some ways you are tempted to forget or ignore the doctrine of inherited sin in your parenting? Think of a time when you didn't take it into account. How might remembering your children need a new heart have changed that interaction?
2. As you look back at your parenting, why have you at times settled for behavior change instead of heart change? How will understanding that we are shepherding our children's hearts change the way you parent your children?
3. List at least three lessons you've learned from reading this chapter and how you will apply them in your life this week.
4. Make a list of other topics you would like to discuss with your spouse, a loved one, friend, mentor, or study group after reading this chapter.

Chapter 3

A Road Map for the Journey

Principle: If we are to raise our children in a way that honors God, parental direction should naturally give way to personal responsibility as they mature.

As a doctoral student, I rarely turned down an opportunity to preach. I already had a sense that the Lord had called me to be a pastor, but, because of my studies, I wasn't able to serve full time at a church. So when a classmate asked me to fill in as a guest preacher for him for a couple of Sundays while he was out, I immediately said yes. He told me the name of the church and the town it was in. He must have assumed I would figure out how to get there. When that Sunday came around, our family got ready, jumped into our van, and began the hour-long ride to the church. Since it was before our smartphones had the aid of GPS, I mapped out the trip on a website and printed out the directions. After driving for an hour, I realized the directions were inaccurate. We found ourselves driving on a single-lane road. Heading toward us was a farmer on a large tractor, leaving no room for us to go around. We were lost, and we needed help. You should have seen me in a suit and tie, climbing out of the passenger window, asking the farmer for directions to the church. He had never heard of the church but was vaguely familiar with the area, so he pointed us in the general direction. Once we came to a corner with a convenience store, we stopped to confirm our directions. The store clerk had never heard of the church, either, but he too thought he knew where the area of the church was. Finally, after driving around for almost two hours, we found the church. The service had already started. A deacon met me outside, gave me the microphone, and I walked directly up to the pulpit to preach. Needless to say, my heart was pumping so hard it felt like it was going to come out of my chest. My nerves were a wreck. But by God's grace, I made it through the sermon.

Parenting can be a lot like our family's drive to this church. We have a general idea of where we're going. We think we've mapped the course. Then we quickly realize things are not going as planned. We keep getting pointed in a general direction, but we're never quite sure we're headed the right way. And finally, we arrive at our destination. Our children are now adults, and we're left wondering, *Did we take the right path? Will he be OK? What if we did everything wrong?!*

Jeanine and I wrote this book not because we have all the answers but because we've been on the road for a while now. By God's grace, we've come to a place where we've given some of our girls away in marriage. Now we are seeing the fruit of grandparenting. We're not experts. We are fellow travelers on the road called parenting. We too have taken a few wrong turns and even exited the highway at the wrong place. But our God is gracious, and we want to keep reminding you of that. God does not expect us to be perfect parents. They have a perfect Father in heaven, and they have a perfect Savior in Jesus. What they need from us is to be humble, repentant, faithful, and godly parents. Don't be discouraged by your failures (we serve a God who makes beautiful creations out of our messes), but know that God's grace does not excuse us from our responsibilities. Before we get into the biblical practice of Christian parenting, we want to lay one last foundation stone in this chapter.

So far, as we have been laying the biblical and theological foundations for Christian parenting, we argued in chapter 1 that our desire for our children should be the same as our heavenly Father's. Then, in chapter 2, we made it a point to remind ourselves that unless we realize that we're parenting in the context of the fall, the best we'll be able to do is modify our children's behavior.

Now, we want to provide a road map to your destination. It's frustrating to know where you're going but not know the road to get there. We'll offer detailed directions for each age group in the final chapters, but right now, we want to give you a bird's-eye view of the road. As you raise your children in the discipline and instruction of the Lord, parental direction should naturally give way to personal responsibility as your child matures through the various ages and stages of life. In other words, when your children are young, you will provide clear and firm direction, but as they grow in wisdom and experience, you will free them to be responsible for their choices. Let's see if we can explain it better by first showing you what happens when you take the wrong path.

The Child-Centered Home

Many Christian parents are familiar with Proverbs 22:6: "Train up a child in the way he should go. Even when he grows older he will not abandon it" (NASB). The original Hebrew reads, "Train up a child *in his own way*,"[3] which seems to mean something different. We need to be careful with this frequently quoted proverb; as one commentator notes, it has "some built-in ambiguities" that we need to be aware of so that we aren't too rigid in the way we apply it.[4] How do you train a child in his own way? The sense of Proverbs 22:6 is that parents should consider their own child in parenting—his own way. God has made each person uniquely and wonderfully. We are to train our children in a way that honors God, while also taking into account their individual personalities, needs, and abilities. That is the way of wisdom that leads to life.

Of course, our sovereign Father in heaven also uses means to bring children to himself. He calls us to raise our children "in the training and instruction of the Lord" (Ephesians 6:4). Imagine if we left our children to their own devices and allowed them to raise themselves. Without our direction, our children will tend to follow their own sinful path. That is the path of foolishness that leads to death. When we allow our children to rule our home, we are actually training them in self-centeredness. Naturally, when they don't get their way, they will become angry. And if we allow children to do whatever they want all their lives, even when they are old, they will not depart from that path. This is what we call a child-centered home. Let us picture it for you in a rectangle:

Figure 3.1 The Child-Centered Home

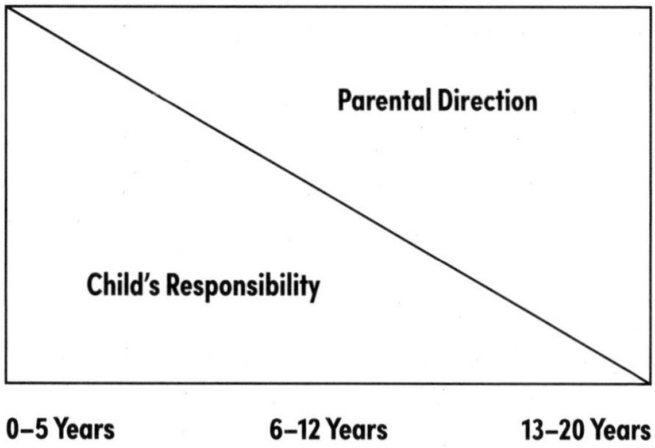

In a child-centered home, parents give their authority away. Notice in the diagram how the parents have given the child a lot of freedom early on. Often, parents don't realize they're doing this. They start by giving the child lots of choices. But giving their child choices grows into letting their child be in charge. Before you know it, the child is running the household. Everything centers on the child. She determines the family menu. He determines when his bedtime is. She determines what family activities you will do. You get the picture. What was once cute—the way she crinkles her nose and tells you no when she doesn't get her way—becomes unbearable by the middle years. Without correction, her "no" becomes firmer with age. Used to getting her way, she becomes angry when you try to correct her defiance or disagree with her choices. Before you know it, you have so trained her in independence that you know things must change. Sadly, it seems it's too late. You've already trained her *in her own way*. In this home, the early years were "fun and cute," but the parents come to despise the "teenage years." Having given so much freedom for most of their child's life, they now feel like they must put on the brakes.

Of course, there is one potential extreme in the child-centered home, and that is that the parents never try to regain control or give direction. In such extreme cases, the children raise themselves without parental direction. Regardless, the child-centered home is usually marked by chaos in the early years and conflict in the later years. But that's not the only wrong path to take as parents.

The Democratic Home

The democratic home is only slightly better than the child-centered home. Democratic parents see themselves as enlightened and civilized. Their aim is to teach their children to make responsible choices, so they set out early on to equip their children to weigh all their options and make wise choices. Then, when it comes to the household itself, decisions are made jointly. Family meetings are organized. Everyone takes turns sharing their opinions. In this home the parents are not the authorities, per se; they are more like facilitators. Here's what a democratic home may look like.

Figure 3.2. The Democratic Home

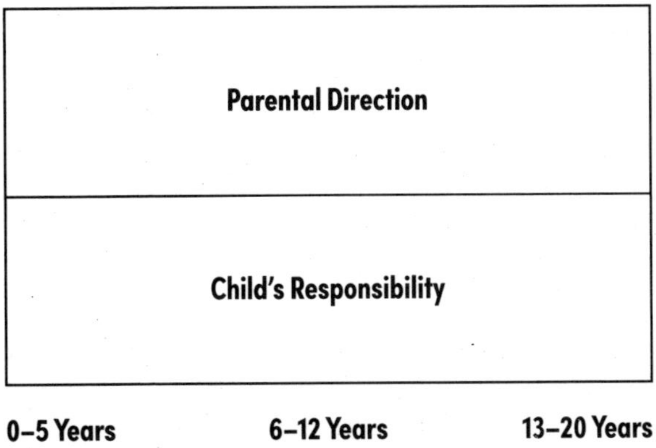

The problem with the democratic home is that it is too naive. It fails to take into account that we're parenting after the fall. And like the child-centered home, it gives the child too much freedom and responsibility in the early years. Here's what I mean: will you "vote" on what will be served for dinner? How will you negotiate what the child will wear for a formal occasion? Will Mom and Dad's votes count double? What happens when the children outnumber the parents? And what about corrective discipline? What will it look like? Will the family sit down every time a child does something wrong and discuss it together? Again, this would be wonderful if it worked, but it fails to account for sinful human nature. So, what should we aim for? What's the path that will help us reach our destination as parents: our children's hearts?

The Parent-Directed Home

In the parent-directed home, the parents seek to represent God's good authority to their children. They embrace authority as a good gift from God, not something to be rejected or embarrassed by. They see themselves as instruments of our heavenly Father, called to shape their children into the image and likeness of the beloved Son. To be sure, these parents aren't perfect. In fact, they know they're not. So, they trust the Lord with all their hearts and see parenting as a lifelong stewardship. In other words, they know they are parenting for the long journey. What might this parent-directed home look like?

Figure 3.3. The Parent-Directed Home

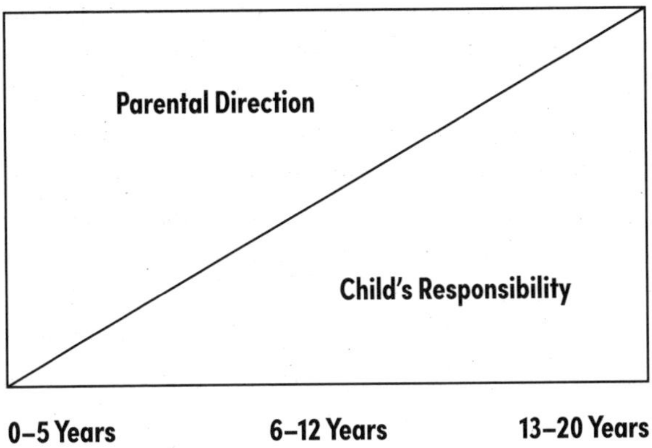

Notice how in the early years there is a lot of parental direction. But, as the child grows in maturity, parental direction naturally gives way to the child's responsibility. While this road map will prove fruitful in the long run, it's not just pragmatic. We believe it is biblical. Throughout Scripture, God warns and encourages his people to stay on the path of righteousness that leads to life. This is a prominent theme in the wisdom literature of the Old Testament (Psalms, Proverbs). In fact, Psalm 1 announces this theme at the beginning of the Psalter. And in the New Testament, this theme is highlighted by the word *walk* (Ephesians 4:1; Colossians 1:10). God has placed all of us in relationships of authority and submission, so that those who are over us may lead us on the right path. As parents, that's the responsibility God has given us for our children.

In Ephesians 6:1, for example, Paul commands children to "obey your parents in the Lord, because this is right." I take Paul to be addressing Christian children in the church. He is, after all, writing to the entire church as Christians, and he commands the church's children to obey "in the Lord." Paul adds, "Honor your father and mother, which is the first commandment with a promise, so that it may go well with you and that you may have a long life in the land" (vv. 2–3). The fifth commandment was given to Israel, and they were to teach their children to honor their parents (Exodus 20:12). This commandment offers a promise: long life in the Promised Land. Under the old covenant, this promise was related to the inheritance of the land. But under the new covenant—that's us—it relates to our eternal inheritance of the new heavens and new earth (1 Peter 1:4). You can't earn an eternal inheritance by obedience. By training our children in the Lord's discipline and instruction, though, his Word (his moral standard) exposes their inability to obey, showing them their sin and pointing them to their need for the gospel. Biblical parenting prepares our children to hear the gospel in the hope that they will one day embrace it. Remember that only God can give your child a new heart. But if he does, their Spirit-empowered, faith-fueled obedience will be a fruit of their salvation.

So, to direct our children on the path that leads to life, we are commanded to "bring them up in the training and instruction of the Lord" (Ephesians 6:4). We'll unpack what that means in the next few chapters. The point we're trying to make in this chapter, though, is clear from this passage. As Christian parents, our God-given role is to faithfully disciple our children toward Christlike maturity. God desires that we would have godly offspring, and parents are the primary instruments God uses to bring our children to himself. The parenting road map God has given us is one in which we direct our children early on. As they mature, though, we are to equip them to handle more and more responsibility. Our aim is that, by the time our children leave our home, they are mature adults who look like Christ and are walking on the path that leads to life.

Do Not Provoke Your Children

Of course, we too are sinners in need of grace and repentance. So there will be times when we frustrate our children. That's why Paul warns us, "don't stir up anger in your children" (Ephesians 6:4). Pastor John MacArthur explains that Paul "suggests a repeated, ongoing pattern of treatment that builds a deep-seated anger and resentment that boils over in outward hostility."[5] Thankfully, our children are resilient and forgiving. But an ongoing pattern that causes a child to feel ashamed, enslaved, belittled, or ignored will lead to building resentment, anger, and eventually, bitterness. How might we stir up anger in our children? Well, there are two overarching dispositions. If you're like us, you oscillate between the two.

1. *The Domineering, Oppressive Parent.* This parent craves control. It is likely that this parent sees himself or herself as following the parent-directed model. And yet, this parent's direction is domineering, controlling, and demanding. It's possible that this parent may seek to maintain control throughout a child's entire life. In such a home, children will feel like slaves. They will suffocate under such control. How may domineering parenting manifest itself? The parent seeks to control their child's actions, their child's behavior. In your situation, you might find yourself saying, "because I said so," often not allowing discussion or explanation. Or it could be that you value your name or reputation so highly that you care more about what other people think about you or your child than how your child matures. So you find yourself regularly repeating threats to try to control your child's behavior. This is a temptation I battled when I was a pastor. We didn't want our children to feel the burden of being responsible, based on their behavior, for what people thought of me or my ministry. I knew that if I wasn't careful, I would try to control my girls for my name's sake, not Christ's. But this is just one extreme.
2. *The Passive, Permissive Parent.* This parent tends to crave comfort or ease. He or she is more concerned with staying in bed in the morning, or watching a show at night, or getting work done during the day, so when the child seeks attention or needs help, the parent puts him in front of the television or hands her a handheld video screen. This

> parent is too self-absorbed to be concerned with what a child is doing or where a child has gone. In many cases this parent is just too busy. Too busy with work. Too busy with church activities. Too busy with friends. Too busy with hobbies. Or maybe this parent just wants the child as a best friend. This parent has this fantasy that just giving children whatever they want and letting them do whatever they prefer will mean children love their parents more.

Of course, I'm purposely laying out two extremes. There is a spectrum between these two poles. And, like I mentioned already, the truth is that we likely go back and forth between the two. Still, there are any number of ways these two sinful parenting dispositions manifest themselves.

1. *Overprotection.* Are you an overprotective parent? Say your children are on the playground, playing on the monkey bars. What's going through your mind: *Ugh, I hope they don't fall*? That's natural for any parent. But the key is what happens next. Do you let your children fall and scrape their knees, or do you hover around them continually so they don't fall? Maybe you don't let your children do anything you think is unsafe. As your children grow up, are you still going to try to protect them from everything? If you hover over your children continually, you'll frustrate them, and they won't be able to learn to do things on their own. When children feel suffocated like this, they can't wait to be old enough to leave home.
2. *Too Much Freedom.* Maybe you prefer to raise free-range kids. In the United States, in an effort to protect animal life, some fast-food companies promise to purchase only free-range chickens. Those are chickens that have not been raised in cramped conditions. Instead, they've been allowed to roam free. When parents do this with their children, they fall into the opposite error of overprotection.

Their children roam free, and they don't concern themselves enough to know whether those children are safe or not. "They'll live," those parents say to themselves. "Children need to learn from their mistakes," parents rationalize. Children under these conditions may grow up to be tough, but they'll also grow up to be too independent. And it's likely they may be frustrated because their parents are never around. As a parent, you may think your children want such freedoms. But from your children's perspective, they are starving for parental attention and care. Know this: if you don't give your children attention, someone else will.

3. *Overly Strict.* Perhaps you're too strict. You're like the first-century Pharisees. You add rule upon rule upon rule that you yourself could not follow, but you expect your children to obey. I'm a parent. I understand legalism. Legalism is attractive. Legalism is easy because you don't have to think. *If you put enough rules around your child,* you think, *they'll turn out exactly how you want them to.* But what if, instead, you crush your children under your rules? What if you exasperate your children into despondency because they just can't obey? Or worse, what if your children are good at rule-keeping, and they become self-righteous, obnoxious little Pharisees?

Like I said, there are any number of ways we stir up anger in our children. Are you harsh in your discipline? You've decided you're going to have a disciplined family. Part of the problem with this kind of parenting is that you give the same punishment for everything. Everything is a capital crime, so everything deserves the most severe punishment. The danger with overly strict discipline is that it can be indistinguishable from abuse. Such harsh discipline may appear to obtain the desired behavior, but it will either push the child into despair or rebellion. Maybe you don't even care about discipline. *They'll figure it out,* you hope. The problem is that our children need boundaries, direction, and discipline. Without them, a child will grow insecure. Ironically, direction and discipline communicate love. Or perhaps you put unbearable expectations on your kids? Maybe you wanted to be the famous soccer goalie, and you just missed out. But if it's up to you, your son will fulfill your dream. So, from age six months, you play ball with him, then in a few years he's enrolled in football camp, and you've already selected his future team. Or maybe you wanted to be a famous musician. So you buy your child an instrument, and insist he practices several hours a day. You take your child to recitals and concerts but may fail to realize he's miserable. You see, it's often the things we were unable to achieve in our youth that we try to impose on our children. Our children are likely to cave under such pressures to perform. Or maybe you have no expectations at all. Do you know what happens when you don't have expectations for your children? They will meet them.

Because we are sinners also, we need to hear Paul's warning: "Fathers, don't stir up anger in your children" (Ephesians 6:4). If I just described you in any way, and the Holy Spirit has convicted you, that is a good thing. Repent. Turn away from your sin. Confess your sin before the Lord. Or maybe your spouse has talked to you about your sinful disposition. Listen to your spouse. If your children have come to you and have tried to tell you that this is what it's like to live under your roof, hear them out. You're not perfect. You still struggle with sin. But our God is a gracious God. Run to him. He desires godly offspring, and he is conforming you to look like Jesus.

Before moving on to the next chapter, you may need to sit down with your family. Gather them together, and ask your children, "When it comes to our family, is our home characterized more by criticism or by affirmation/encouragement?"[6] Then let your children speak. Hear their words. I understand they may not have a full understanding of all that is happening in your life, especially the younger they are. But listen to them. I'm not a hunter, nor do I even own a gun. But I have gone target shooting before.

My aim was to hit the bulls-eye. Since I'm not a great shot, I would often hit the target somewhere around the bulls-eye. That's how we should listen to criticism. Maybe what your children will say will miss the bulls-eye, but if what they're saying is somewhere on the target, then it's likely something you need to deal with. Be sure to make your home a safe place for them to respectfully express their opinions. And make sure your home is a safe place to confess sin. Lead by example. Apologize when necessary. Ask forgiveness when you sin. And always be ready to grant forgiveness when sinned against. Then be thankful. Thank God that your children are willing to help you grow in the grace and knowledge of Christ.

And ask for help from people outside your family. You don't have to walk on this parenting journey alone. Think about other families you admire. Invite them to dinner. Glean wisdom from them.

If you've realized your shortcomings after reading this chapter, don't be discouraged. Our Lord is incredibly patient and forgiving, and so are our children. So, don't put off having important conversations that will help you get back on the right path. Our children need our direction. They need us to direct them on the path that leads to life. And God, in his wisdom, has given them you to lead them.

Conclusion

When I was seventeen years old, I enlisted in the United States Navy. During my first year, I attended a school for potential officer candidates. Our company was led by two United States Marines: one a staff sergeant who fought in Vietnam, the other a sergeant who served in Force Recon. Needless to say, we did everything with discipline. When I returned to university to complete my undergraduate degree, I was different from other college students. I ironed my clothes. My hair was short. I was physically fit. Essentially, while no longer actively serving in the Navy, I still had a military mindset. I brought that mindset into our marriage and into my parenting. As our children matured in our home, and they began to communicate verbally, I barked out orders. I was the captain, and our home was my ship. Everyone in our house was under my command. I expected the children to be bathed, their dress to be neat, and the house to be in order. Then, one day, after I came home and gave orders, Jeanine pulled me to the side and asked, "Do you want a home that can be featured in a magazine, or would you prefer to have a relationship with your daughters?" In my mind, I thought, *Why can't I have both?* Jeanine graciously pointed out that my children were afraid of me. I was a stranger in my own home. My children viewed me as an authority who gave orders. Of course, if you failed to complete those orders, you would be brought before the military tribunal of one: me!

I thank God that Jeanine loved me enough to point out my sinful parenting disposition. I was frustrating my children. I was frustrating my wife. On the outside all looked well. But at home, I was losing my children. Because of my wife's love and care, I realized I needed to change. I needed to be characterized more by encouragement and affirmation than by criticism and correction.

Some of you can relate to my desire for order. Others will err in the opposite direction. Because all of us are imperfect, we need to be humble as we grow and learn as parents.

One of the great lessons we've learned over the years is that if we were going to raise our children in the training and instruction of the Lord, we needed to lovingly direct them in the younger years and teach them how to take personal responsibility as they matured.

Thankfully, our kids don't need perfect parents. They have a perfect Father in heaven, and they have a perfect Savior in Jesus. What our children need us to be is faithful, humble, repentant parents who love them as our heavenly Father loves us. May our homes be safe places for our children to grow and even to fail. May our homes be welcoming and loving, so that our children want to be there and even bring their friends. And may we lead our children by example and instruct them from God's Word, that God would save them and cause them to grow up in the Lord to be godly.

Talking Together

Perhaps this chapter, more than the others, has caused you to think about your own parenting. Maybe the Lord has used it to bring about conviction. If so, that's a good thing. Our aim is not to discourage you or for you to see yourself as a failure. Our aim is to point you to the heavenly Father, who is perfect, and who is ready to forgive his repentant children. Additionally, our God has given us a road map to direct our children on the path that leads to life. After reading this chapter, get with your spouse, a faithful friend, or a group of parents and discuss the chapter. Here are some questions to get you started.

1. After reading this chapter, identify which parenting road map you've been following. Did anyone point you in this direction? Or is it what has come naturally to you?
2. As you think of ways we tend to stir our children to anger, were you able to see yourself in any of the descriptions? What are some ways you stir your children to anger? Do you need to ask your children to forgive you?
3. What are some steps you can take to start using the right road map to lead your children on the right path?
4. Make a list of other topics you would like to discuss with your spouse, friend, or discussion group after reading this chapter.

[illegible] ...

[illegible] the doctrine of inherited sin, we will often [illegible] to change our children's hearts in our own [illegible] might be trying to change your child's heart if you [illegible] with them to obey for reasons other than [illegible]

[illegible] find yourself saying things like, "Honey, please [illegible] the past ten minutes. I'm just [illegible]

[illegible]

[illegible] behavior for a brief moment [illegible]

[illegible] into account. How might [illegible] your children need a new heart have changed [illegible]

[illegible] look back at your parenting, why have you at times [illegible] for behavior change instead of heart change? How [illegible] understanding that we are shepherding our children's [illegible] change the way you parent your children?

[illegible] three lessons you've learned from reading this [illegible] and how you will apply them in your life this week.

[illegible] Make a list of other topics you would like to discuss with your spouse, a loved one, friend, mentor, or study group after reading this chapter.

Chapter 4

The Place of Spiritual Warfare and Faith-Fueled Prayer in Raising Children

Principle: Faithful parenting engages us in a spiritual battle for the hearts of our children that must be undergirded by faith-fueled prayer.

Parenting is war! Now, don't get me wrong. I know it sometimes feels like we're at war with our children. But that's not what I mean, because that should never happen. What I mean is that parenting is a spiritual war for the hearts of our children. In Ephesians 6:10–18, the apostle Paul prepares us to face this war.

> Finally, be strengthened by the Lord and by his vast strength. Put on the full armor of God so that you can stand against the schemes of the devil. For our struggle is not against flesh and blood, but against the rulers, against the authorities, against the cosmic powers of this darkness, against evil, spiritual forces in the heavens. For this reason take up the full armor of God, so that you may be able to resist in the evil day, and having prepared everything, to take your stand. Stand, therefore, with truth like a belt around your waist, righteousness like armor on your chest, and your feet sandaled with readiness for the gospel of peace. In every situation take up the shield

> of faith with which you can extinguish all the flaming arrows of the evil one. Take the helmet of salvation and the sword of the Spirit—which is the word of God. Pray at all times in the Spirit with every prayer and request, and stay alert with all perseverance and intercession for all the saints.

While Paul applies his exhortations to the whole of the Christian life, I will focus our application directly to parenting. If we are to raise our children in the face of the temptations that confront us all from the world, our own flesh, and the devil, we must be strengthened, stand firm, and suit up.

Be Strengthened!

As with any war, we will need strength to engage and endure. Faithful parenting is exhausting work. At times we will wonder if we have the strength to keep going. So Paul commands, "Be strengthened" (v. 10)! He's not asking us to find inner strength. To do so would be disastrous and lead to defeat. No! The command is in the passive voice. That is, it is a command to receive strength, which means finding strength outside of ourselves. But from where? Verse 10 tells us: "by his vast strength." Literally, in the "strength of the Lord." That's good news! Take heart, Mom. Do not fret, Dad. The Lord provides the strength we need to fight our sin, defend ourselves from Satan's darts, and raise our children according to God's desires. We are weak. He is strong. We are dependent. He provides everything we need to be faithful parents. It may not seem like it at times, but the strength the Lord provides is "the mighty working of his strength" (Ephesians 1:19). This is the same power that raised Jesus from the dead. And that is the strength at your disposal, Christian. Resurrection power! But how are we to be strengthened with this power? That's a great question, leading us to what Paul commands next: "Put on the full armor of God" (v. 11).

Suit Up!

We find our strength in the Lord by putting on his armor. Take note: we are to don God's armor, not ours or some other armor. Too often, in both the Christian life and in parenting, we look for strength and protection in persons, things, and places other than God. We seek strength to parent our children in experts, professionals, schools, government, methods, or programs. But when we put our hope in anything other than the Lord, we are like Israel's kings who looked to other kings and their armies in their times of trouble. Instead, we must seek our strength in the Lord by putting on his armor. As the Psalmist declares, "Some take pride in chariots, and others in horses, but we take pride in the name of the Lord our God" (Psalm 20:7).

We need God's armor to "stand against the schemes of the devil" (v. 11b). There are two important things to note: first, the devil schemes. If you're familiar with the Bible, this comes as no surprise. Our introduction to the devil or Satan, the serpent of old, comes when he works to deceive Eve in the garden of Eden. Jesus called Satan "a liar and the father of lies" (John 8:44). In the heat of parenting, Satan will tempt us to believe lies about ourselves—"You're a bad parent"; "You can't keep going"; "Your child hates you." And he will tempt you to believe lies about your children—"They're awful"; "They never listen"; "There is no hope." Another helpful way of thinking about the devil is as a master counterfeiter. He offers competing (counterfeit) promises to lure us and our children away from the path that leads to righteousness and life. And he uses various means to accomplish his ends: the world, our own flesh, and his direct action. In the book of Revelation, we learn that he uses corrupt government, false religion, and ungodly culture. That's what we're up against. That's what our children are up against. And we need God's armor to combat his schemes.

Notice, second, that it is the devil who is our true enemy: "For our struggle is not against flesh and blood, but against the rulers, against the authorities, against the cosmic powers of this darkness, against evil, spiritual forces in the heavens" (v. 12). If we're not careful, we will think of other people—unbelievers, political officials, teachers, entertainers, influencers (flesh and blood) as our enemies. It is especially dangerous when we are tempted to view our children as the enemy. We don't ever want to get to a place where we think it is them versus us. Remember what Paul says: we are not fighting against flesh and blood. My spouse is not the enemy. My children are not the enemy. We are fighting against the devil and his forces as he works to undermine our marriages, our parenting, even our faith. The devil is organized and scheming against us. Satan will use whatever methods are at his disposal to steal, kill, and destroy! So don't give up any ground.

Stand Firm!

We put on God's armor so that we may stand firm against the devil (v. 13). This is the emphasis of the passage (see vv. 11, 13, 14). We're not commanded to win the battle. Jesus has already done that by defeating Satan through his death and resurrection. Our job is to stand firm—to not lose ground to the enemy. How? Again, by putting on God's armor.

We stand firm against the devil's schemes first by standing on the truth of the gospel (6:14a). When Satan tempts you to believe parenting is hopeless and your child will never respond, remember the glorious gospel of grace. We, too, were once dead in our trespasses and sins, but God made us alive in Christ (Ephesians 2:5). If God can save and change us, he can save and change our children. Remember that Satan is a liar and the father of lies. He attacks through deception, but we are armed with God's truth. The image of truth as a belt around our waists pictures how a Roman soldier would ready himself for battle. This leather belt went under his armor. It gathered his tunic, so that he would be free to move. We ready ourselves for battle with the Word of truth. It is in this truth that we were sealed with the Holy Spirit when we believed (Ephesians 1:13). And it is this truth we are to speak to one another in love to help one another grow in Christlikeness (Ephesians 4:15). The truth of which Paul speaks is in Jesus (Ephesians 4:21), and it is recorded for us in Scripture. So, we prepare for battle against Satan and his schemes by knowing the truth that is in Jesus. That means reading, studying, and memorizing Scripture are wartime activities that prepare us for spiritual battle. Personal devotions are a wartime activity by which we prepare for spiritual battle, and if we are to be strengthened in the mighty strength of Jesus, we must be dependent on him. We must spend time with him. We must be in communion with him. Speaking the truth in love to one another (discipleship) is also a wartime activity. Husbands and wives need to encourage one another with the truths of the gospel. Single parents need to encourage one another with the truth that is in Jesus. We all need to build one another up. And we also need the church. Gathering with the church to read, pray, sing, hear, and preach Scripture is a wartime activity by which we prepare one another for spiritual battle. For this reason, in chapter 6, we will talk about the place of biblical instruction in raising children. But our battle is not just about knowing the truth; we must also live it out.

Second, we stand firm against the devil's schemes by walking in righteousness (v. 14b), which Paul pictures as a breastplate. The breastplate protects the chest and heart. Walking in righteousness protects us from Satan's schemes, the world's influences, and the temptations of our own flesh. In Christ, we are new creations, being "created according to God's likeness in righteousness and purity of the truth" (Ephesians 4:24). We grow in righteousness and holiness as we put off the old self and put on Christ (Ephesians 4:20–24). In other words, we stand firm against the schemes of the devil when we pursue righteousness in the Lord's strength. It is important to remember that our children are watching us. They hear what we say and see what we do. We are instructing them by our lives. This is why, in chapter 5, we will discuss the place of godly example in raising children. When we are empowered by the Spirit with the knowledge of the truth and we walk by faith, we can walk in a manner that pleases the Lord (Romans 12:1–2).

Third, we stand firm against the devil's schemes by proclaiming the gospel (v. 15). The shoes or sandals that the Christian soldier wears are the gospel of peace. The image comes from Isaiah 52:7, "How beautiful on the mountains are the feet of the herald, who proclaims peace, who brings good news of good things, who proclaims salvation, who says to Zion, 'Your God reigns!'" Satan seeks to blind unbelievers to the truth of the gospel. He disguises himself as an angel of light to deceive. But Jesus will build his church through the preaching of the gospel. This is good news! Our unbelieving children are blinded to the truth of the gospel through Satan's lies and their own hard hearts. Thankfully, the Lord has placed them in our homes so that they may see and hear the gospel. Sharing the gospel with and teaching the gospel to your children is a wartime activity. Jesus came and preached peace to all, to both Jew and Gentile (Ephesians 2:17). And this is what we are called to do in the Great Commission (Matthew 28:19–20). And, of course, sharing this good news begins at home. Moms and dads, don't underestimate the daily conversations and teaching opportunities you have with your child. Only God can save, but he delights in saving his children through human instruments who regularly and faithfully share the gospel.

Fourth, we stand firm against the devil's schemes by protecting ourselves with the shield of faith (v. 16). The fight against sin and temptation is a fight of faith. Satan bombards us with arrows and missiles to get us to doubt God—particularly to doubt God's sovereignty, wisdom, and goodness—and to doubt ourselves—our faith, our parenting, and our motives. Faith in God and his promises protects us from Satan's attacks. When we believe Jesus—his Word, his promises, his warnings—the devil's arrows will have no effect. We will stand firm against Satan.

Fifth, we stand firm against the devil's schemes by remembering our salvation (v. 17a), which Paul calls a helmet. The helmet protects the head—our thinking. Satan tempts us to doubt and despair over our salvation—to undermine our assurance. But we have been united with Christ and receive all the spiritual blessings of the salvation he has planned, accomplished, and applied to us (Ephesians 1:3–14). God chose us before the foundation of the world. Imagine. He knows everything about us, and he still loves us. He justified us by faith in Jesus, and we've received forgiveness of sins as a result. That means we are not justified by our parenting. If God has justified us, no one can condemn us, not even for our parenting. God has adopted us in Christ. That means no one or nothing can separate us from God's love for us in Jesus—nothing, no affliction or conflict, no success or failure, not even if our adult children reject Christ and his ways! "If God is for us, who can be against us" (Romans 8:31 ESV)? Therefore, because we are in Christ, a future inheritance awaits us. When we have confidence in God and his saving grace, we will stand firm against the devil.

Sixth, we stand firm against the devil's schemes as we use Scripture against him (v. 17b). The sword of the Spirit is the only offensive weapon named in God's armor, and it is the Word of God—the truth, that is, the gospel. We combat Satan and his schemes by standing firm on the Word of God. This is how Jesus battled Satan in the wilderness. And this is why Scripture memorization is so important. Again, we will consider the importance of Scripture in chapter 5. And remember that we do not fight with our own strength. That means we must depend on God. And that means prayer.

Pray!

Finally, we stand firm against the devil's schemes as we pray (v. 18). Prayer is not part of the armor. It undergirds it. It is a means by which we are strengthened in the Lord as we draw near to him in our time of need. We pray because we are in a battle for the hearts of our children, and we are powerless to change their hearts. Only God can do that. So we pray. We cannot produce guaranteed outcomes through parenting formulas or practices. So we pray. We are helpless to parent in our own strength. So we pray—at *all* times, in the Spirit, with *every* prayer and request, staying alert with *all* perseverance and intercession for *all* the saints (v. 18). Prayer is a wartime activity. As John Piper reminds us, prayer is the wartime walkie-talkie we use to call out to God for air support in the heat of the battle.[7] Consider how we may pray for ourselves and our children.

At all times in the Spirit

Parenting requires praying all the time and at all times. By "all the time," we mean that we are to be in a continual state of prayer—structured, unstructured, spontaneous, and planned. During our regular times of planned prayer, we are drawing near to our God, and he is drawing near to us. And we pray that God may grant us to be strengthened with the Spirit's power to know and experience Christ's love for us (Ephesians 3:14–19). That regular communion with our Lord Jesus Christ strengthens us for what we may face that day. We should also offer what I call "arrow prayers." When King Artaxerxes learned of the returned exiles' situation and asked Nehemiah what he wanted to do, Nehemiah prayed to the God of heaven, then answered the king (Nehemiah 2:4–5). There will be times in our lives as Christians and as parents when we will need to shoot an arrow of prayer to heaven in the heat of the moment. Every time the Lord brings our children to mind, we should pray for them. In the midst of a parental crisis, we should pray. When our children are facing a challenging situation, we should pray. And most times we should include our children in those prayers.

We should also have planned times of prayer for our children. Jeanine and I prayed regularly for our children during our personal devotions. We've done it in different ways over the years. Sometimes we used prayer cards for each child. At other times we made lists with specific requests. The point is that, in whatever way works best for you, you should pray regularly for your children. And don't only pray *for* your children. Also pray *with* your children. For our family, our regular prayer time was during breakfast. After our morning Bible reading and discussion, we prayed together. We taught our girls early on to fold their hands and listen. We invited them to share their prayer concerns and needs as they grew older. Eventually, we all shared prayer requests and took turns praying for one another.

One of the sweetest prayer times I remember was at bedtime. Since Jeanine stayed at home with the girls during the day, I took responsibility for our evening and bedtime routine. Once each of the girls was in bed, I would kneel by their bedsides in turn, invite brief encouraging conversations, sing three songs (the same three songs every night), and pray for them. At bedtime I would often pray for their salvation in their hearing. I would ask the Lord to replace their hearts with new hearts that would beat for him so that they would run hard after Christ all the days of their lives. I miss those evenings now that they are all adults.

Praying at *all* times means we pray in *all* circumstances—whenever a need arises. I prayed when they were away from us. I prayed when we were away from them. I prayed when they were driving. We would pray as we began a road trip together. We prayed when they were sick, when they were having a hard day, and in all kinds of circumstances. No matter what we may face, we express our dependence on God when we are on our knees and relying on the Spirit's help.

With every prayer and request

Parenting also requires that we pray all kinds of prayers. As a parent, we may have some prayers that we pray regularly, but as all kinds of challenges arise in our children's lives, we also pray all kinds of prayers to meet the need of the moment. We pray for their salvation first and foremost. We pray for their health. We pray for their growth in grace once they are believers. We pray that they would do their best in school. We pray for a godly spouse. We pray for a stable job. Yes. We're always praying about all kinds of things. There is nothing too trivial to bring before our loving Lord. And there is nothing too big for our Creator God to handle. So, we bring every prayer and request to him, because he cares for us and he cares for our children.

With all perseverance and intercession

Parenting requires that we pray for our children with all perseverance. The weightiest prayers require perseverance. Our youngest, Maxey, was diagnosed with juvenile idiopathic arthritis in the middle years. It was a challenging journey for Jeanine, me, and Maxey as the doctors suppressed her immune system in an effort to reboot it. As of today, she is twenty years old and has failed every medication she has tried. On a scale of one to ten, with ten being the greatest pain level, she lives her life at a six. I've pleaded with the Lord to heal her. I've asked the Lord to allow me to be sick instead of her. But the Lord, in his wise providence, has allowed her to bear this burden with us at her side. Still, we persevere, interceding for her healing. And the Lord has taught us that the answer is yes. Maxey will one day be healed. We pray it will be soon, but it may be when she receives her resurrection body. Regardless, the Lord has promised that one day she and all of us will be made new.

Conclusion

Mom and Dad, we do not parent in our own strength. We parent in the Lord's. And we are commanded to be strengthened in the strength of the Lord. How? By suiting up in God's armor. He has provided everything we need for life, godliness, and parenting. So as we raise our children in a manner that brings him honor and glory—in the discipline and instruction of the Lord, hoping one day he will save them and conform them to the image of his Son—we do so in the same power that raised Jesus from the dead. Now, as our children are confronted by the temptations of the world, their own flesh, and the devil, we stand firm in the Lord Jesus Christ. You see, to put on the armor of God is another way of saying we are to put on Christ (Romans 13:11–14). Jesus has already won the victory, and we stand firm in his strength, giving up no ground to the enemy. That is the war we call parenting. So Mom, Dad, be strengthened in the Lord's strength! Suit up in God's armor! Stand firm on the truth of the gospel! And pray—at all times, in all ways, with all kinds of prayers!

Talking Together

Do you now have a better understanding of parenting as a spiritual battle for the hearts of our children? I wonder if we often find ourselves exhausted in parenting because we are trying to do it all in our own strength.

1. How does thinking about parenting as a spiritual battle for your children's hearts change your perspective about parenting? How might it change your approach to parenting?
2. Where have you been looking for strength to endure in parenting? What will you do now to seek the strength of the Lord?
3. What role does prayer play in your parenting? How do you pray for your children? How often? What kinds of prayers? What changes do you think you need to make to your prayer life to be strengthened by the Lord and show your dependence on him?
4. After reading this chapter, what would you like to discuss further with your spouse, friend, or discussion group?

Chapter 5

The Place of Parental Example in Raising Children

Principle: If we are to raise our children in a way that honors God, the truths of the gospel must, first, be on our hearts and, second, be lived out before our children.

Grandparents do silly things around their grandchildren. Just think about the way they talk. The faces they make. The things they do. When you see your own parents behave that way you wonder, *Who are these people?* Well, Jeanine and I are at that fun stage now, and we find ourselves doing some silly things just to make our grandchildren laugh. We also enjoy getting to know them as they grow through the various stages of development. One of my favorite stages is when toddlers begin to mimic you. Our almost one-year-old granddaughter is at that stage. If she is in the right mood, when we laugh, she laughs. When we cough, she coughs. When we move our hands a certain way, she tries to do the same. It makes for fun play times and wonderful memories.

When your children begin to mimic your actions and sounds, parenting becomes more fun. Recently, I was on the floor playing with my two-year-old granddaughter, when I got a cramp in my leg. I let out a pained sound and laid out on my back to stretch my leg. What did she do? Laugh, of course. Then she lay down beside me and held her leg just like me. Clearly, we have to be careful, because when children learn to copy what you're doing and saying, they will copy you when you don't necessarily want them to. This fun game of copycat points to an important parenting principle we need to embrace: even before our children understand any instruction we provide with our words, they are receiving instruction when watching what we do. The old saying is true—actions speak louder than words. This is the next parenting principle we want to consider: *if we are to raise our children in a way that honors God, the truths of the gospel must first be on our hearts and, second, be lived out before our children.*

The Power of Parental Example

When I was young, my dad smoked several cigarettes a day. Personally, I hated the smell. Since my dad smoked, though, I thought it was cool. Naturally, I wanted to be like my father. So, I found a cigarette, borrowed a lighter, and hid in a corner. Being only six years old, my skills at operating a lighter were not strong. No matter how hard or how often I rolled my thumb across the striker to ignite the flame, nothing happened. Still, I must have made enough noise that a hand came down from heaven (so it seemed), picked me up by my shirt, and carried me through the air. It was my dad. It all happened so fast. Immediately, I knew I was in trouble. I never lit the cigarette, and to this day, I've never smoked. But as a six-year-old boy, I wanted to be just like my father. I had watched him smoke all my life to that point, and I wanted to smoke—just like my father. Such is the power of parental example.

Our children will mimic what we do—both good and bad. If we want to raise children according to God's desire, we must provide a godly example. This is not to say that they will become godly by just watching us. Remember that they are born with hard hearts. They need new hearts. Still, by design, God has established that our children want to be like us, just as we were created to be like our heavenly Father. Let us, then, work to provide a godly example for them to follow.

The experience of Paul's young friend Timothy shows us that even though living a godly life before our children will not guarantee their salvation, it does provide a powerful example of living faith before them. Just think of the way Paul speaks about Timothy, his "dearly loved son" in the faith (2 Timothy 1:2). Timothy was a man of faith, but Paul remembers that this "sincere faith" first lived in Lois, his grandmother, and Eunice, his mother (2 Timothy 1:5). Single parents, take encouragement from Timothy's testimony. Timothy's mother was a believer, but his father was not (Acts 16:1). Yet, the example of faith in his mother and grandmother left a profound impact on Timothy. How do we know? Because Paul reminds Timothy of this godly example, saying, "You know those who taught you, and you know that from infancy you have known the sacred Scriptures, which are able to give you wisdom for salvation through faith in Christ Jesus" (2 Timothy 3:14–15).

But Paul goes even further. He charges Timothy to continue in what he has learned and believed on the basis of his knowledge of those who taught him—his knowledge of their words and their lives (2 Timothy 3:14). One of the examples Paul appeals to is his own. As a disciple of Paul, Timothy had followed Paul's "teaching, conduct, purpose, faith, patience, love, and endurance, along with the persecutions and sufferings" (2 Timothy 3:10–11). Paul's point is simple. In the context of the church in Ephesus, where he is being challenged by false teachers, Timothy is to pursue godliness and maintain a faithful gospel ministry by remembering the example of those who discipled him. By following their example and their teaching, Timothy will fight the good fight "as a good soldier of Christ," "compete as an athlete" without being disqualified, and receive his reward like "the hardworking farmer" (2 Timothy 2:3–6).

As you can see, the concept of imitation is thoroughly biblical. We are called to imitate our Father in heaven, walking in love and forgiving one another as we have been forgiven in Christ (Ephesians 5:1–2). We are warned against imitating evil. Instead, we are to imitate what is good because those who do good are from God (3 John 1:11). And, of course, Paul is not shy about asking his disciples to imitate him (2 Thessalonians 3:7, 9). As Christians, we are even called to imitate our pastors: "Remember your leaders who have spoken God's word to you. As you carefully observe the outcome of their lives, imitate their faith" (Hebrews 13:7). If we hope to impress upon our children that God is glorious and that Jesus is beautiful, the truths of the gospel must first be in our hearts, and they must be lived out before our children.

The Root of a Godly Example

You cannot pass on what you do not have. Your children will see what flows out of your heart in good times and bad. And they will follow whatever example you give them.

Remember Jesus's words in Matthew 15:18–19:

> "But what comes out of the mouth comes from the heart, and this defiles a person. For from the heart come evil thoughts, murders, adulteries, sexual immoralities, thefts, false testimonies, slander."

Whatever is in our hearts will flow out into public view. And whatever our children see from us, they will want to imitate—at least while they're young.

Providing a good parental example requires intentionality, and providing a godly example requires a new heart. Consider the Lord's words to Israel as they prepared to enter the Promised Land. He commanded Israel to pass on the words of the Sinai covenant to their children: "The LORD our God, the LORD is one. Love the LORD your God with all your heart, with all your soul, and with all your strength" (Deuteronomy 6:4–5). And notice what God said next: "These words that I am giving you today are to be *in your heart*" (Deuteronomy 6:6, emphasis added). You cannot pass to your children what you do not have. Moms and dads, if you desire to raise your children in the discipline and instruction of the Lord, you must pursue godliness yourself. The truths of God's Word must first be on your hearts.

Have you repented of your sins and trusted in Christ alone for your salvation? New hearts are our (and our children's) greatest need. And the fulfillment of that need is one of the great promises of the new covenant. The Lord declares, "I will put my teaching within them and write it on their hearts" (Jeremiah 31:33). Unlike the covenant at Sinai, where God's teaching was written on tablets of stone, the new covenant Jesus initiated by his sacrificial death promises that our hearts of stone will be replaced with hearts of flesh that beat for God (Ezekiel 36:26). We are also promised God's Spirit dwelling in us (v. 27). While, under that old covenant made at Sinai, God directed his people through leaders who had the Spirit, another great promise of the new covenant is that all God's people will have God's Spirit (Joel 2:28–29).

If you're a Christian, God has given you a new heart and made you alive in Christ by his Spirit to walk in the power of a new life (Romans 6:4). This is what our children need from us as parents—for our hearts and lives to mirror to them this new life we have in Christ. As those who are made new, we are to walk in the good works that "God prepared ahead of time for us to do" (Ephesians 2:10). That is, we are to walk in a manner that is "worthy of the calling" we have received (Ephesians 4:1). We do that as we grow in the grace and knowledge of Christ by his Word and Spirit, with the help of the church (Ephesians 4:11–16). God's aim for us is to be godly, that is, to look like his Son, who looks just like his Father in heaven. Jesus is the true image of the invisible God, and he is producing godly offspring by his grace, through his gospel, and in the power of his Spirit. And we, who have the privilege of raising children in a Christian home, have the same aim—to raise our children to look like Jesus.

This is a great tension in Christian parenting. We cannot guarantee our children's salvation by our godliness, but God has placed them in our homes to witness the love of the Father and the gospel of his Son in us. Just as Israel was to display their God to the surrounding nations, and just like the church displays our King and his kingdom to an unbelieving world, so too parents display the love of the Father and the goodness of his gospel to our unbelieving children. But to do that faithfully, we must be ones in whom the divine image is being renewed. That is, these words must first be in our hearts. With new hearts and God's Spirit indwelling us, we are empowered to live as godly examples before our children.

The Practice of Godly Example

Here's the point: your children are watching you. They're always watching. So we must be intentional about the example we live before them. That includes every area of our lives. But we want to highlight three broad areas for you to focus on. You may need to consider these areas anew or just pay more careful attention to them. Since laying a biblical foundation is the most vital of these three areas for raising godly offspring, we'll start there.

Model personal devotion to God

God did not send his only begotten Son into the world to save us just so we could escape judgment. He saved us to bring us into relationship with himself, through his Son, by his Spirit. We are saved to be in fellowship with the triune God, the Creator of all things! He is our Father. We are his adopted children by faith in Jesus, our Elder Brother. And he invites us to commune with him. How? God has revealed himself to us throughout history in his words and deeds and ultimately in his Son (Hebrews 1:1–4). By the ministry of the Holy Spirit, what God wants us to know about himself and his works has been written down for us in Scripture (2 Timothy 3:16–17). That means we know and commune with God by reading and praying over his Word, with the help of the Spirit.

Do you spend time with God in prayer, reading his Word, seeking his guidance by his Spirit? If it's not currently a part of your regular life, commit to reading and studying the Bible. Give yourself in prayer to the Lord. Ask for the Spirit's help. We have found it most helpful to establish a time, choose a plan, and find a place for our personal devotions. Sitting in the same place, at the same time, with the doable plan, has helped us develop habits that became normal and natural.

For many years of my parenting life, I (Jeanine) was instructing my children in something I didn't consume daily. I knew enough Bible to point out specific passages when my children misbehaved. But I was malnourished, not taking in a nutrient-dense diet of God's Word daily on my own. After being transparent in a mentoring relationship about my lack of personal devotions, another mother and I began holding each other accountable for spending daily time in the Word. Sadly, I had believed the lie that as an exhausted mom of several young children, it was understandable that I did not have time to carve out for this. I thought it was enough that I prepped to teach others, went to church, and listened to praise music. That sounds like enough, doesn't it? The problem was that I wasn't being still and meditating on God's Word for my personal benefit. For my personal holiness. At the heart of it, I was believing the lie that I didn't have time and that I was fine without consistently spending time in God's Word. I wasn't an awful person. I wasn't a bad parent. I wasn't an unfaithful wife. Still, I had to assess my own heart, and I came to the realization that I had to love being in God's Word more than sleep. That was the personal sacrifice I had to make. Remember my friend I was mentoring? We decided to call one another each morning to make sure we were up and had done our devotions. There was no texting at that time. Only a loud landline in the early morning. That's what it took to begin this spiritual discipline in my life.

I wish I could tell you that this time in God's Word has been a spring of flowing water for the last twenty-five years. It hasn't always. In fact, it's still hard at times, but that's why it's called a spiritual discipline. I often have to reorient my thinking and remind myself that being in God's Word is better than ________. You have to fill in the blank for yourself.

But this isn't just for moms. Dads, you too must be in God's Word if you are going to lead your family in godly living. This is one of the most common complaints I hear when I sit down with frustrated moms: their husbands aren't leading their family in God's Word. There is no shortcut to personal holiness. God has revealed himself by his Word, and if you want to meet with God, you must read his Word. Spending time in God's Word is not only food for your soul, but it also provides a great example for your family as you meet together for family devotions. The main point we want to stress is the importance of knowing God's Word so that you may know God. This is our aim—to know him that we may become like him. When the truth of God's Word is in our hearts, we can pass it along to our children. But we must also lead our children by the example of our actions.

Model personal holiness

Speaking about pastoral ministry, the Scottish pastor Robert Murray M'Cheyne (1813–1843) is known to have said, "My people's greatest need is my personal holiness." Pastors must, of course, stand on the truth of God's Word. But we cannot separate life from truth. This is why Paul warned Timothy, "Pay close attention to your life and your teaching" (1 Timothy 4:16).

It's no different in our homes. Our children's greatest need is our personal holiness. And yet, it seems like the family is the most difficult context to be holy in. Let's consider just a few of the difficulties we may encounter as parents.

"Mean what you say, and say what you mean." Jeanine encouraged me with those words on more than a few occasions. That's because, after a long day of work, I would get home, and the girls would ask me for something or to do something. In my selfishness, I would stall, offering to do it later. Yes, I was exhausted, but my girls hadn't seen me all day. "Let's go ride bikes," they'd suggest. "Tomorrow," I'd respond. "Let's go to the park," they'd suggest. "Tomorrow," I'd say. Then the inevitable would happen. Tomorrow became today. "Remember what you promised," Jeanine would remind me. On the days when my delay tactics were successful and the girls forgot, it was not a win for me or for them. It was a promise unkept. In those moments, I was not showing them the truth about our heavenly Father. He keeps every promise he has ever made. I am thankful for Jeanine's continual encouragement. She didn't nag. She simply reminded me to "mean what I say and say what I mean." Of course, there are other ways we confuse our children.

Young people are smart. They can spot hypocrisy immediately. As parents, we find ourselves in this dilemma far too often. It's more comfortable to point out hypocrisy in others. Think about that family at the grocery store. You know the one. The parents are shopping, and their child is out of control. Juanito is touching every single item on the shelves. He's not staying close to his mother, and the beautiful pyramid displaying his favorite snack will come tumbling down if he pulls out the box within his reach. It's like the game Jenga but with groceries. So how do the parents respond? They lose their minds. Naturally, they're frustrated. I would be too! But rather than shepherding their child's heart, they give him a tongue lashing. "Juanito, don't touch that! Stay away from there! Come back here!! Quit touching everything!!!!" Surely, we can empathize with the flustered parents. What you may not recognize, though, is the hypocrisy in this situation: the parents are asking the child to exercise self-control, while they have just lost theirs. That's what lashing out in anger is—a lack of self-control in dealing with a situation that displeases us.

Instead, if the parents had provided a godly example of self-control, they would have helped equip their child for success—at least in the long run. Time and time again, we want to equip our children for success in challenging situations, and our godly example will go a long way in doing that. That way, we can continually point them to Christ in us. So, what if the parents had approached it this way: "Juanito, we are about to go into the grocery store, and I know how you struggle with touching things on the shelves. I am allowing you to take your truck (or favorite item) with you to hold so you can keep your hands busy. Remember what Mommy expects. Please do not touch anything, or you will lose the freedom of walking by my side." There you go! You have set the expectations. Now, when Juanito obeys, you may affirm his obedience. But when he disobeys, which he will when you begin training him, you don't have to lose your temper. You can show self-control in how you respond because you have a plan.

Or think about parents of teenagers. Perhaps you've heard this comment: "Show me some respect! When you roll your eyes and storm off, that's disrespectful!" If you're the parent of teenagers, then you know the battle—the battle for respect. All you want is for your children to speak to you kindly, for them to share their feelings with self-control, and for them to do the simple tasks you ask of them. Where did they learn disrespect? Could it be that they have been under your tutelage for over thirteen years, watching how you respond to your spouse? They hear you say things like, "You have no idea what you're talking about," or "Why did you do _______?!" Do you find yourself arguing with your spouse in front of your children? If you do, then don't be surprised when your children respond to you in the same way. Do you belittle your spouse in front of your kids? Then don't be surprised when your children do the same thing. What about when your spouse makes a decision you may disagree with? Do you undermine it by criticizing your spouse to your children? Or, how about when your spouse establishes a punishment? Do you go behind his/her back and let your child know that you'll "take care of it," so the child gets her way? Your deceptive examples are showing your child that manipulation works. It shows them that if you disagree with a decision someone makes, you can still work at getting your own way. Don't be surprised when your child uses the same manipulative tactics that they've observed in you. Don't be shocked when your children pit you against your spouse when they don't get what they want.

Model having difficult conversations

Another important example we can provide our children is the way to have difficult conversations. No one likes to have them, but they are necessary if our relationships are to flourish. We must have difficult conversations at church, at work, and at home. But do you allow your children to have hard conversations with you? Do you welcome your teenager saying things like, "When you speak to me like that, it makes me feel dumb." When they are thinking through worldview issues, do you allow them to admit, "I don't think I see it that way, Dad." When they come home from school, are they able to tell you, "You never let me go out with my friends, and I feel like I live in a jail." Why do your children feel like they live in a jail? Have you practiced allowing your children to safely say things you don't like and then calmly discussing the issue at hand?

I cannot sufficiently stress the importance of this exercise, this habit. Strong relationships are built on trust, and that requires fostering trust over time. In forming a friendship, you go out to dinner and play games together, just to get to know one another. Then you find yourself sharing parts of your life, your struggles, with the person to see if it is safe to share. Can you trust the person? Strong family relationships require the same sort of trust building. Your children have a lot bottled up inside of them: some of it safe and easy to share, and some not so safe. They will not reveal to you their struggles if you haven't already done your "battle for relationship." Are you safe? Have you led by godly parental example to allow them to share how they feel about life, about your relationship? Juan led our family by opening up potentially challenging conversations, many times around the dinner table—a great way to get indigestion at times. It always made me nervous because I wondered what our children would say. The topics for these family meetings varied, but one question was asked regularly: "Do you feel that Mom and Dad are your greatest cheerleaders or your greatest critics?"

When your kids are mad at you and spout off things that are hurtful like, "I feel like I'm in prison," stop, pray that arrow prayer, and assess if you should overlook it in the moment and wait to respond or address it immediately. When you're ready, revisit it and ask open-ended questions like the following: "What do you mean when you say that? Why do you feel our family might be that way?" And then ask clarifying questions such as these: "Can you give me an example of that? What does that look like to you?" Here's the hard part—listen! No talking. No defending yourself. Just listen. Then in humility, say, "I'm sorry I have made you feel that way. Thank you for sharing that with me. Can I share with you why Dad and I made that decision?" Or if, after a healthy conversation, you realize it was the wrong decision, simply admit it.

When modeling how to have godly conversations, especially when we disagree with one another or when the topic is difficult, no conversation topic should be off-limits. None! Because if your children can't talk with you about sensitive topics, they will find someone else to talk with. If you're unwilling to listen to them, they will find someone who will. And that someone may not point them to Christ. As our children grow, they will face the normal questions children have about God, themselves, family, life, death, and everything in between. Add to that the questions the culture is forcing them to ask—questions about sex, gender, violence, politics, war, poverty, discrimination, climate change, and the list only grows. We know it's hard being a parent, but imagine how hard it is being a child in this cultural climate.

Clearly, our conversations with our children should be age appropriate. With girls, talking about their bodies is extremely important. I'm sure it is with boys too, but we've found that girls tend to have a lower self-image than boys. I (Jeanine) was convinced it was important to talk about the way God made our bodies without tying everything to sex. But when it was time to talk about sex, we didn't make it a big deal. Yes, it's special, but I didn't need to drop $1,000 on a special getaway weekend to talk about it. When we came across terms and situations in Scripture, we discussed them. Simply. Respectfully. Naturally. There were times it was appropriate to say, "That's a great question, and when you get a little older, we will talk about that." And we did. Even in the midst of challenging conversations, we sought to preserve the dignity of our children by answering no more and no less than was helpful.

Your kids will ask questions, hard questions. They are seeking answers to things that matter to them. When your preschooler wants to talk nonstop, welcome it. When your middle schooler is bothered by a kid at school, listen. When your child likes another student but gets rejected, give that child your shoulder to cry on. When your children tell you they are depressed and hate life, hold them. That they want to share with you is an honor and privilege. When your children come to you wanting to share their hearts, don't brush them off. Don't panic. Don't avoid them. Don't overreact. And don't try to solve all their problems. Sometimes they just want to talk. And when they raise a complaint about you, don't become defensive. Hear them out. They may miss the bull's-eye, but ask yourself if they're hitting the target somewhere. As you listen to your children, you will earn their trust. And when you've earned their trust, you will enjoy many conversations that will knit your hearts together. For the last thirty years our girls and I (Jeanine) have talked about things that have humored me, hurt me, and scared me. But through those conversations, we have built lasting relationships. And this, my friends, is a mercy of God.

Model seeking forgiveness

Speaking of hard conversations and doing hard things, what if we modeled the humility of a teachable spirit before our children? We value it in our children and even our spouses! Have you ever walked away from a conversation where you have confronted children about their sin and you were amazed at their response? They took ownership and listened thoughtfully, possibly even asking clarifying questions. Sounds like a dream, doesn't it? How about when your child sins against you and asks for forgiveness? As parents, we need to be modeling these qualities. There were several practices that were important in the Sanchez household, including asking for forgiveness and having hard, respectful conversations where all people could share their thoughts in a safe environment. And these things started with us as parents.

We weren't perfect parents. We sinned against each other. We sinned against our children. We lost our tempers. We became exasperated with our kids. We were lazy at times and put our own needs first. Parenting is sometimes overwhelming, especially when you're dealing with multiple children at once. I found myself having to referee many verbal conflicts. "She stole my doll! She took my jeans!" On one occasion, in my haste, I disciplined the wrong child. I listened to the loudest one and just wanted to be done with it. I had more important issues to deal with! Afterward, another child (remember that there were five of them) came forward with the whole story. I had to humble myself and not just apologize but ask for forgiveness. I had to model what I had taught my girls for years. "Zoe, I'm sorry for disciplining you wrongly," I had to confess. "I didn't listen to the entire story, and that was wrong of me. Will you please forgive me?" Thankfully, children are resilient and forgiving. She happily and freely granted me forgiveness, and the relationship was restored. By God's grace, we witnessed the fruit of parental example that day.

Conclusion

As we think about raising children in a Christian home, we cannot minimize the impact a godly example can have on them. They're watching us—how we talk, how we treat people, how we work, and how we recreate. Because we were created to be like our Father in heaven, we were created with a bent toward imitation. Children want to imitate their parents. So let us give them a worthy example of personal devotion to our Lord because God's Word is in our hearts. And let us live our lives before them in such a way that they may glorify our Father in heaven on the Last Day.

Talking Together

This may have been a tough chapter to read. You may be discouraged, because you feel you have not provided the best example for your children. Remember that confession of sin and asking for forgiveness are a good and godly example for our children. That may be where you have to begin. As you think back on this chapter, talk to your spouse, your friend, or to the people you're reading this book with, and talk about the kind of example you're providing your children.

1. What kinds of examples did you have growing up? Which examples were most encouraging to you? Why?
2. How are you encouraged by the example you are living before your children?
3. What are some areas in which you need to grow as you consider being a godly example before your children?
4. Is it possible that you need to ask forgiveness from one or more of your children for being a bad example in a particular area? What does repentance look like in that situation? Don't be afraid of admitting your sin, first to God, and then to those you've sinned against. Our tendency is to cover up our sin, like our first parents, Adam and Eve. However, God promises that if we uncover our sin before him, he will cover it in the blood of his Son. Take a moment to read and meditate on Psalm 32.
5. What are some steps you will take, beginning today, to live in the power of the Spirit, in obedience to God's Word, in order to live as a godly example before your children?
6. Make a list of other topics you would like to discuss with your spouse, loved one, friend, mentor, or group after reading this chapter.

Chapter 6

The Place of Biblical Instruction in Raising Children

Principle: If we are to raise our children in a way that honors God, we must teach them the truths of the gospel from God's Word, using biblical methods to reach biblical goals.

It was a normal evening. Jeanine and I were leading our girls through our bedtime routine. Each night we aimed to read a few Bible story books, work through a catechism, and pray. We only had three girls then, and the youngest was about two and a half years old. At the end of our routine that night, Jeanine took the two older girls to brush their teeth. I found myself alone with our youngest. We had been reciting the catechism with the older girls while she was with us, but I began to wonder what would happen if I asked her those same questions. So, with just the two of us in the bedroom, I asked Question 1: "Who made you?" I assumed that would be the end of it, but without missing a beat, she responded in the best way a two-year-old can, "Tod made me." Intrigued, I asked Question 2: "What else did God make?" She said, "Tod mad all tings." Now utterly stunned that our two-year-old had been following along during our catechism time, I asked her Question 3: "Why did God make you and all things?" To my amazement, she replied, "Por his own tlory."

That evening I learned an important parenting lesson. Actually, two. One—routine faithfulness is never a waste of time.

Two—children can remember and learn a lot more than we realize. Don't underestimate your children's ability to receive and remember instruction. Children are like sponges. They are always learning. And, if you don't teach your children, someone else will—extended family members, neighbors, peers, or television programs. So make sure you're the one teaching your children!

But let me offer a warning. As I learned with our youngest daughter, our children are always learning, even when we don't realize we're teaching. And if we're not careful, we will teach our children the wrong things because we're unintentional about what we teach or shortsighted in our goals. Here's what I mean. You're in a public setting, and your children are running wild. People begin looking at you in judgment, and you're embarrassed and frustrated. What happens next is important. Too many parents in that situation simply want their children to stop, sit down, and be quiet. Those aren't unreasonable goals, but if the only instruction your children receive happens when they misbehave, you will fall into the trap of becoming just another threatening parent who repeats the same commands all the time— "Stop! Sit down! What's wrong with you?!" If we fail to instruct our children positively, our homes will be characterized by "No," "Stop," and "Don't." Or maybe, instead of the threatening, repeating parent, you are the bribing parent. You offer your children prizes to follow your instruction. You might bribe them with a toy, a treat, or screen time on their favorite device. You want them to behave at the grocery store, so you say, "If you behave while we are here, I'll get you some candy at checkout." That's bribing. Remember that our goal is not behavior modification. We want to reach their hearts with the truth of the gospel and point them to the One who gives a new heart and the indwelling Spirit who empowers obedience.

Here's the warning: *unbiblical parenting goals will lead to using unbiblical parenting methods.* Read that again. It's that important. And unbiblical methods will result in frustrating our children. They will be frustrated because we're asking them to follow rules without an understanding of grace and the gospel. Or, worse, we will create little Pharisees who understand neither grace nor the gospel but are good at following the rules. They just want the prize at the end. Could it be that one of the reasons a large number of children who grow up in the church leave the faith is that they have been led to unbiblical goals with unbiblical methods that result in a hypocritical Christianity that must be rejected?

In 2 Timothy 3, Paul appeals to Timothy: "But as for you, continue in what you have learned and firmly believed" (v. 14). And he gives Timothy two reasons for continuing in the instruction he had received: (1) because he knew from whom he had learned it (v. 14)—the importance of biblical example and (2) because he had been instructed in these things since infancy—biblical instruction. In chapter 5, we focused on the importance of biblical example for parenting. In this chapter, we'll focus on the importance of biblical instruction. If we are to raise our children in the training and instruction of the Lord, we must teach our children the truths of the gospel from God's Word, using biblical methods to reach biblical goals.

The Content of Biblical Instruction

The Bible must serve as the foundational text for instructing our children. That sounds obvious, but it needs to be said. Because we're always teaching and our children are always learning, if we don't intentionally ground our instruction in God's Word, we will ground it in something else. Sometimes we will default to what our parents did. Too often, we will follow the latest trends or do what our peers are doing. Instead, in 2 Timothy 3, the apostle Paul reminds us why the Bible must serve as the foundation for our instruction. In the Bible alone we find "the sacred Scriptures, which are able to give you wisdom for salvation through faith in Christ Jesus. All Scripture is inspired by God and is profitable for teaching, for rebuking, for correcting, for training in righteousness" (2 Timothy 3:15–16).

Why the Bible and not just general moral instruction? Because only the gospel is "the power of God for salvation" to all who believe (Romans 1:16). Moral instruction may help us teach our children how to behave or respond in certain situations, but it cannot change the human heart. Remember that that's the human problem, and that's the problem our children face—apart from Christ, their hearts are hard and naturally rebellious. But God has chosen to change human hearts through the power of the gospel. And this gospel is revealed in "the sacred Scriptures" (v. 15). The sixty-six books that compose the Christian Scriptures, our Bible, are divinely inspired and the basis for Christian instruction. The Bible must be the foundational text for instructing our children.

The source of our instruction will also determine the goal of our instruction. And the goal of our instruction is that our children would receive new hearts and be formed into the image of Jesus. And the means by which God removes hearts of stone and replaces them with hearts of flesh is the new birth, which comes about by the power of the Spirit giving life through the gospel word (1 Peter 1:23–25). That's what Paul means when he tells Timothy that these sacred Scriptures "are able to give you wisdom for salvation through faith in Jesus Christ" (2 Timothy 3:15). How will our children receive new hearts to be able to hope in God apart from the good news of Jesus? They won't. The Spirit does not grant life apart from the word of truth (James 1:18). The best they'll be able to achieve apart from Christ is to be well-behaved.

Even when someone receives a new heart and becomes a follower of Christ, though, that person still needs to grow in wisdom and knowledge in regard to their faith. This same gospel which is the power of God for salvation to all who believe is also "profitable for teaching, for rebuking, for correcting, for training in righteousness" (2 Timothy 3:16). In other words, the Bible is beneficial for teaching truth and refuting error. It is beneficial for correcting unrighteous behavior and training in righteousness. It is God's Word to us. And because it is God's Word, we receive it as true, authoritative, and without error.

So we must teach the gospel, revealed in the Old and New Testaments, not only that our children may come to know Christ, but also that they may grow to look more and more like him. This is not just the aim of biblical parenting; this is the aim of biblical discipleship. And that's what parenting is all about. That means that the Bible, not a parenting book, not even this parenting book, is the foundational source for parental instruction. Our aim in writing this book is not to presume we've figured something out others haven't. It isn't to pretend that if you follow our approach, your children will turn out perfectly. No! Our aim is to point you to the One who changes hearts and gives grace and accepts us as we are in order to change us to look like him. That is our only hope. Understanding God's grace in salvation as revealed in the Scriptures will help you persevere through your parenting journey—that understanding is your compass that points you back in the correct direction.

So you must teach your children the gospel at every opportunity. *You* must be the primary discipler of your children. Too often, parents drop off their children at the church nursery or Sunday school class, expecting that they will learn about Jesus there. Some parents may enroll their children in a private Christian school, hoping that they will learn about Jesus there. While those opportunities may be good and helpful, God has given *you* the primary responsibility for raising your children in the training and instruction of the Lord (Ephesians 6:4). So allow your church's children's ministry to reinforce your own discipleship at home, but don't let that be the main source for your child's discipleship. Feel free to enroll your child in a private Christian school if you can afford to, but don't expect that your children will grow in Christ there. God has designed the family as the primary place for the discipleship of our children.

So, at home, spend more time reading books that point to our Savior than you do reading books about superheroes and wild animals. Choose books for your children that exalt Jesus more than those that exalt your children. Remember that the content of biblical instruction is the Bible. And since young children can't read, you should prioritize reading age-appropriate books to them that summarize Bible stories. Read the Bible together as a family. Again, you will be surprised how much children are learning. In our home, we read the Bible while eating breakfast together before I left for the office. That was the time we could be most consistent. During that time, I would read from a translation of the Bible that was easy to understand. The girls were encouraged to ask questions about the passage, and I would ask them how I could pray for them. We prayed together, and then we were ready for our day. It was that simple, and therefore easy to be consistent. In the evenings, we sat together after dinner and spent the time before bed reading aloud, reciting the catechism, and praying together. That was how we tried to begin and end each day. You don't have to do what we did, but you do have to teach your children God's Word. To do that, I suggest you find a rhythm that works for you. Talk to other parents. Ask your pastors. Consider your daily routine. And account for your work schedule. The best rhythm is the one that works for you and your family.

A Model for Biblical Instruction

Remember that our children don't need us to be perfect. They need us to be faithful. And part of being faithful is diligently instructing our children in the Word of God. To do that, we need to establish a plan for biblical instruction. The key to such a plan is to keep it simple and remain consistent.

So, commit yourself to the Lord and begin instructing your children, however old they may be. How might you begin? New parents, especially, will be tempted to think that their infant is too young to learn. But remember the pattern God laid out for Israel after the exodus:

> "Listen, Israel: The Lord our God, the Lord is one. Love the Lord your God with all your heart, with all your soul, and with all your strength. These words that I am giving you today are to be in your heart. Repeat them to your children. Talk about them when you sit in your

> house and when you walk along the road, when you lie down and when you get up. Bind them as a sign on your hand and let them be a symbol on your forehead. Write them on the doorposts of your house and on your city gates." (Deuteronomy 6:4–9)

Not only were the words of God to be on the parents' hearts (vv. 4–6), but they were also to teach them to their children diligently (v. 7). How? "Talk about them when you sit in your house and when you walk along the road, when you lie down and when you get up" (v. 7). In other words, the words of God that are on our hearts are to continually roll off our lips as we are walking to the park, shopping at the grocery store, making their beds, or teaching them to ride a bike. These regular Scripture-saturated conversations should characterize our biblical instruction.

Also notice the importance of writing Scripture down and having it serve as a reminder to obey God and keep the covenant. God told Israel to bind his Word "as a sign on your hand and let them be a symbol on your forehead" (Deuteronomy 6:8). To honor this command, the Israelites wrote down important Scripture passages and, literally, wore them on their hands and placed them on their foreheads in little boxes called phylacteries. The symbolism served as a reminder that what God's people do with their hands and think with their minds is to be controlled by the Word of God.

Deuteronomy 6:9 reminds us that God's people were also to write Scripture and post it around their homes and even at the gates of their cities. Take a moment to walk through your home. What is hanging on your walls? Is there a theme? What are you celebrating? It's not wrong to celebrate family and your children's accomplishments, but keep in mind that what you hang on your walls and place on your refrigerator—those are the things you are celebrating. Those are the things you want people to know about your family. Those are the things your children will remember were important to you. The Israelites were to post Scripture throughout their homes. It would be wise for us to do the same.

Choose Scriptures that are central to the Bible's storyline. Choose Scriptures that glorify God's work in Christ. Choose Scriptures that offer prayers or invoke blessings for your family, and post them in appropriate places throughout your home. Write Scriptures on Post-it notes and place them in your children's rooms or on their bathroom mirrors. As children grow up in a home that is saturated with Scripture, they will remember what was important to you. They will look back on key Scripture verses, and, we pray, they will remember your God.

A Plan for Biblical Instruction

To see what healthy biblical instruction might look like, consider Psalm 78:1–8:

> My people, hear my instruction;
> listen to the words from my mouth.
> I will declare wise sayings;
> I will speak mysteries from the past—
> things we have heard and known
> and that our ancestors have passed down to us.
> We will not hide them from their children,
> but will tell a future generation
> the praiseworthy acts of the LORD,
> his might, and the wondrous works
> he has performed.
> He established a testimony in Jacob
> and set up a law in Israel,
> which he commanded our ancestors
> to teach to their children
> so that a future generation—
> children yet to be born—might know.
> They were to rise and tell their children
> so that they might put their confidence in God
> and not forget God's works,
> but keep his commands.

> Then they would not be like their ancestors,
> a stubborn and rebellious generation,
> a generation whose heart was not loyal
> and whose spirit was not faithful to God.

The historical setting for this psalm is the decline of Israel due to their disobedience and covenant breaking. If they continue down this path, they will receive God's judgment. The question Israel faces is how they will stave off disaster. The answer? Psalm 78 looks back at Israel's disobedience throughout their history to warn the present generation and encourage them to instruct their children in the ways of God. If Israel forgets God—his ways, works, and words—they will no longer believe in God, they will continue the path of rebellion, and they will receive God's judgment. For this reason, they must instruct their children in the ways, works, and words of God. Psalm 78:1–8 provides a helpful summary of what we're encouraging you to do in this chapter.

As we raise our children in the training and instruction of the Lord, we are leaving behind a confessional legacy. In Psalm 78, the psalmist shares a body of teaching. This body of instruction is what Israel has believed and confessed. And the psalmist wants the following generations to believe and confess these same truths. Every generation is leaving a legacy. We're leaving a deposit of instruction, which the next generation will pass on to their children. We pass on our ethnic heritage, our family traditions, our grandmothers' recipes. Our children will learn to love what we love and learn to hate what we hate. What legacy are you leaving behind for your children? The legacy we pass on to our children will either liberate the next generation or leave them in bondage. What are you leaving behind? What is the content of the beliefs you are passing on to your children?

Notice the content or source of the psalmist's confessional legacy. What he has received and passes on to the coming generations is God's revelation of himself. God has revealed himself in his works and his words. His works—"the praiseworthy acts of the LORD, his might, and the wondrous works he has performed" (v. 4)—reveal his character and power; his words explain his works and reveal who he is. As the psalm unfolds, the psalmist shows us that God is just in his judgments (vv. 21–33, 59–64). God is gracious in his salvation (vv. 12–16, 43–55). God is merciful in his forgiveness (vv. 34–39). God is loving in his guidance (vv. 65–72). All these things the psalmist passes on. How else would the next generation know who God is and what he has done? How else will we learn who God is and what he is like?

Following the example of the psalmist, we are to leave to our children a glorious vision of God—his praiseworthy works and truthful words. How? Teach your children the glorious, praiseworthy work of God, beginning with creation. Children love nature. They love animals. As you teach your children about nature, point to them to the glorious Creator who made all things. When they are babies, we love to teach them all the animal sounds. Do you also, in the next breath, praise God for his creativity in making all those animals? When they grow up, do you marvel at God's wisdom as you discuss the human body and how it works? The more you practice bringing God into these daily, mundane activities, the more it becomes second nature.

As a family with young children, we loved being in nature. Going hiking in state parks, riding bikes, and playing outside were weekly activities. We even ventured on a few camping expeditions. We wanted our children to love being outdoors and to enjoy God's creation. The magnificent rainbow after the rain—God made that. The beautiful waterfall on our hike—God did that. The colorful sunset on a warm summer evening—God is responsible for that. Those were wonderful opportunities to teach our children about God. How are you taking the routine activities of life and using them to praise your Creator? Use every one!

When children sin or are sinned against, teach them about Adam and Eve and how they sinned against God (Genesis 3). Help them understand how we have inherited Adam's sin and now are inclined to sin against one another. And most importantly, use your children's moment of disobedience and discipline to point them to their need of Christ, the beloved Son whom God sent to save us from our sins by dying on the cross and conquering sin and death. That may sound complicated, but it's not really. It might sound something like this: "When you stole your brother's toy while he was playing with it, was that kind? No. It's hard to be kind sometimes, isn't it? Remember when we read about Adam and Eve and how they sinned against God by disobeying him? That also means that we are sinful now, and that makes it even harder for us to be kind. But God loves you and wants to forgive you and help you obey. So tell God what you did wrong and ask him to forgive you. Next tell your brother what you did wrong and ask him to forgive you. Then let's pray that God would help you change your attitude toward your brother." And then we do this repeatedly, encouraging them to identify their sin by naming it and pointing them to Christ, who is their only hope and strength.

Base all your instruction on God's revealed Word, the Bible (Psalm 78:5–6). The most important legacy we leave our children is the vision of God, his praiseworthy works, and his truthful words from Scripture. We recommend considering the following categories of discipleship practices:

1. *Scripture.* If we are to give an overall picture of our glorious God and his praiseworthy works, we must read Scripture together. There is no shortcut to the knowledge of God and his works. He has revealed who he is and what he has done in Scripture. Here are some ways to incorporate Scripture into your children's lives:
    - *Bible Reading.* Select a Bible translation, like the New International Reader's Version (NIRV) or the New Living Translation (NLT), that is easy for everyone to understand. Find a plan for reading the Bible. Choose a time and a place to sit together as a family and read the Bible out loud. You don't have to read an entire chapter. You just need to keep it simple and

be consistent. As your children grow older, ask them questions about what you've read. Again, the key to parental instruction is to keep it simple, be consistent, and consider what is age appropriate.

- *Bible Storybooks.* Especially when children are very young, you may want to read Bible stories from picture storybooks. Find Bible storybooks that are faithful to the biblical message and visually engaging. Small board books are also helpful for children who can't read. You may sit children on your lap and read several Bible board books at bedtime or during a break in the day. We liked to keep a basket of books in our family area. Regularly, the children would choose several books and ask us to read them out loud. As we read to our children, not only are we cultivating a love for God and his Word, but we are also instilling in them a love for reading.
- *Worship Services.* To encourage your children, buy them their own age-appropriate Bible. Teach them how to find the books of the Bible. Help them understand how the Bible is put together into an Old and New Testament. And encourage them to follow along in their Bible whenever the Bible is read out loud or the sermon is preached. For very young children, take out a sheet of paper and give them key words to listen for. When they hear the key word, have them make a check mark next to it. This simple activity teaches children how to listen to sermons.

2. *Prayer.* Prayer is learned by imitation. As your children hear you pray, they will learn how to pray. As a part of your family time, set aside a few minutes to pray together. Pray simple prayers. Ask your children what concerns they have. Pray about those together. Be sure to share family concerns and pray for those. One of the joyous ways children learn about the marvelous, praiseworthy works of

God is through answered prayers. As you share concerns and pray for them, be sure to let them know when God has answered. Here are some great times to incorporate prayer into your routines:

- *Pray during meals.* Teach your children that the food you have is provided by God. And give thanks. This is a perfect time to teach them to pray aloud.
- *Pray at bedtime.* Teach your children that God is everywhere. He hears the prayers of his people. And when we're afraid, we can cry out to him.
- *Pray in times of need.* Teach your children that they can go to God in prayer at any time and especially in times of need. Are they afraid of starting that first day of school? Pray together. Are they concerned because their friend was mean to them? Pray together. Is a loved one sick? Pray together.

3. *Doctrine.* From an early age and in age-appropriate ways, we must prepare our children to understand the truths about God, Scripture, humanity, creation, sin, Christ, the Holy Spirit, salvation, the church, and the eternal kingdom. The following options can be great ways to give your children a solid foundation in doctrine:
   - *Catechism.* A catechism is a question-and-answer method of instruction. It also aids in memorization. You ask the question, and the child responds with the answer. There are a number of historical catechisms you may use, many of which are available in simplified versions and in modern English. The point of a catechism is that it teaches children about God in doctrinal categories. By doing so, it helps children develop a framework for understanding God, his ways, and his works. I (Jeanine) started doing this while changing their diapers. I had a captive audience! I (Juan) then started using bath times to ask the questions—use every moment!

- *Conversation.* As your children mature in age and knowledge, they will ask you many questions about God's character, God's work, the world around us, sin, and Christ. As they do, take advantage of those moments to talk together. Encourage questions. One lesson we learned is to answer only the questions they have, not the ones they are not asking. Doing that may require asking them to clarify what they mean by their questions. Too often, we're answering a question they don't have or offering them information they're not quite ready for. Don't fret when their theology is off, they are confused about God, or they have doubts about the Bible. Just answer their questions with age-appropriate answers and patiently and lovingly point them to the truth that is in Jesus.
- *Creeds and confessions.* The historic creeds and confessions of the church are important summaries of what the church has believed. These documents are not only a good way to teach about the history of the church, but they are also helpful ways to teach doctrines that the church has deemed important throughout its history.
- *Books on doctrine.* The word doctrine means "teaching." By doctrine, I am referring to the essential teachings of the Christian faith. Of course, the source of those teachings is Scripture. So by teaching doctrine, we are helping our children understand how to understand and interpret the Bible. What are those beliefs we want our children to learn? That's doctrine. You don't want all your doctrinal instruction to be reactive—in other words, you don't want only to be correcting their wrong theology. So establish a plan to teach your children about doctrine. Choose a doctrine, like the doctrine of God's sovereignty or the

Trinity, and find books you can read together. This is a great opportunity to learn together!

4. *History.* All history is God's history. We need to help our children understand how God is in control of all history and how he is directing all things to his appointed end. The history we find in the Bible explains how God has been at work in earlier times. It helps our children understand that even in difficult times, God is at work, and we can trust him. Here are some wonderful ways to familiarize your children with historical events:
   - *The Bible.* The Bible is not just a history book, but it does record how God has worked throughout history. It reveals that God is directing history to his appointed end. Teach your children the history of God and his people. This is what the psalmist does in Psalm 78. The history of Israel functions as a parable to warn the coming generations what happens when they forget God (1 Corinthians 10:6).
   - *History books and biographies*: History and biography can be fun reading. Choose time periods and people that interest you and your children. Learn how God is at work in the world and in people. We loved reading missionary biographies with the girls. There are many fun series to read that are very engaging for all ages.
   - *Trips to historical sites*: Often when we traveled with the children, we made it a habit to stop in historical locations to learn about the event or events that took place there. They didn't always appreciate it, but we were hopeful that they would one day! On our most recent trip, we took our three youngest daughters on a trip to Mobile, Alabama, where we learned about the history of civil rights and racism in the United States. This led to many conversations where we could guide

our girls to right thinking and point them to Christ who is gathering diverse peoples and making them one (Ephesians 2:11-22).

5. *Literature.* Good literature can also point us to God and his praiseworthy works. Sometimes literature exposes human depravity and sin. At other times, through stories, we see how God works. For example, one of our favorite read-alouds was John Bunyan's *Pilgrim's Progress.* Through allegory, Bunyan paints a picture of the difficulties of the Christian life and the challenge of following Christ until death. Our girls also enjoyed C. S. Lewis's *The Chronicles of Narnia.* Again, these stories have underlying Christian themes that point to the glory of our God and his praiseworthiness. Switch up the types of literature to keep it fun! Some of our favorites had us laughing in tears, and then crying with sadness. This gave us more opportunities to have life conversations and disciple our girls.

This sounds overwhelming, doesn't it? You might be thinking, *You really expect us to do all that reading?! There's no way!* We all make choices to do what we most want to do—things that matter. Sports are important, so your kids go to practice three days a week. School is important, so they attend classes every day. Biblical instruction is much more important, so carve out time for it. The drop-in-the-bucket mentality works well. We used the end of family meals, bedtime routine, etc., to read. We decided that reading was more fruitful than television most nights, and our girls look back at those reading times as a favorite family activity. It was a sacrifice that bore much fruit.

The Purpose of Biblical Instruction

Stated positively, the psalmist reminds us that the purpose of leaving behind a confessional legacy is "to teach . . . their children so that a future generation—children yet to be born—might know" (Psalm 78:5–6). To what end? "So that they might put their confidence in God" (v. 7). Stated negatively, it was so the children would "not forget God's works, but keep his commands" (Psalm 78:7).

As parents, we must understand the long-term goal of biblical parenting—children who reflect God's image. Again, we cannot make our children believers. We can't change their hearts. But in his divine plan, God has established that he will bring about the new birth "by the word of truth" (James 1:18). So we parents are God's instruments, caring for and teaching the children he has providentially given to us. And our goal is to raise our children according to God's desires. Preach the gospel and paint a glorious picture of our God and his praiseworthy works so that our children may realize their sin, embrace Christ, and put their confidence in God. And pray diligently that God would apply the biblical instruction you provide to the hearts of your children. God is after their hearts, and he is the only one who can change them. By God's grace, when your children come to know Christ, then their obedience will flow from a new heart.

Conclusion

Too often, we're parenting for the short-term. That's to say that our goals are shortsighted. We parent for the moment. When we parent for the moment, we will become frustrated by what our children do now. That's often why we feel embarrassed by our children's behavior in public. They throw a fit. They shout something embarrassing. They inconvenience us. And in that moment, we just want it to stop. So we sacrifice relationship and instruction.

We understand. We've been there. We were at a family wedding—quite a large event—and all our girls (three at the time) were dressed in their wedding party attire. It was time for the reception, and we were walking into a large hall filled with guests. Our youngest started throwing a fit, and we were unable to take her into the ballroom without all eyes staring. We needed to go in there—they were announcing our names soon! Was I (Jeanine) concerned about what was going on with her? Nope. Did I calmly sit with her, giving her tools to learn to control herself? Once again, nope. I sacrificed long-term instruction and relationship for short-term gain. At the heart of it, I wanted everyone to see our pretty little girls and how well-behaved they were. I was short-sighted.

That's a wrong perspective. Instead, we need to remember we are parenting for the long term. We need to parent with eternity in mind. To do that, we need to remember the purpose of biblical parenting. Our aim is to raise our children in the training and instruction of the Lord (Ephesians 6:4), so that they may be equipped for a God-glorifying life of good works through Jesus Christ. To do that, we must paint a marvelous and awe-inspiring picture of who God is for us in Christ, both by godly example and biblical instruction, so that by God's grace, our children would set their hope in God, persevere in that hope, and glorify God by their lives.

Talking Together

Our children should know that our lives revolve around God and his glory! We must pass on to them our great love for God. Do this exercise sometime: ask your children to guess what you love most. What do you think they will say? Your favorite food? Sports team? Your spouse? Or, would they say, you love God above all else? Something or someone will become first and foremost in your children's life—what will that be? What kind of picture of God are you painting for your children?

1. What are some steps you are currently taking to instruct your children in the Lord?
2. If you've not formed a regular habit of biblical instruction, what are some of the first steps you can take?
3. With your spouse, loved one, friend, mentor, or your small group, put together an age-appropriate plan for biblical instruction in your home.
4. Make a list of other topics you would like to discuss together after reading this chapter.

Chapter 7

Biblical Discipline: Leading Children to Walk in Wisdom

Principle: If we are to raise our children in a way that honors God, we must consistently apply biblical discipline, which requires both positive instruction and corrective discipline.

If you were to take the time to sit down and make a list of all the things you wanted to teach your children, it would take days. There are just too many things to cover! I learned this lesson the hard way. One day, when Juan and I were house hunting for a move to a new city, one of the sweet church members offered to take care of our three girls. When we returned, our kind babysitter had a little twinkle in her eye. Naturally, I asked how the girls behaved. Her answer betrayed the reason for her smirk. While preparing lunch, she allowed our youngest to help. That little darling Sanchez was standing on a stool beside her when she leaned back and said, "Mrs. Riddle, you're fat! You have a big bottom." Immediately, my face turned red. I was mortified! My husband was going to be her new pastor! It never crossed my mind to teach our daughter not to tell people they were fat. Thankfully, Mrs. Riddle was kind. She understood the mind of a toddler. Still, it was a reminder to teach our girls how to honor adults and how to model a 1 Corinthians 13 kind of love.

It would have been unwise to discipline our daughter for what she said. We hadn't equipped her for this situation. More importantly, she was not defiant; she was not doing anything we had told her not to do. This experience served as a reminder that our girls needed instruction. We may not be able to teach our children *all* the right things to say or not say in every circumstance, but we can, for example, teach them what Scripture says about our tongues, about kindness, and about wisdom. Clearly, we had a lot of teaching to do! And it will take your child's entire childhood to learn those important lessons.

Over the years, we've learned that biblical discipline requires both positive instruction and corrective discipline. And we need the wisdom to discern when each is required. One reason parents overuse corrective discipline is because they fail to provide positive instruction. We must spend time teaching our children about obedience and disobedience in age-appropriate and developmentally appropriate ways. This is what we mean by positive instruction—teaching obedience and warning against disobedience before it happens. Keep in mind that positive instruction and corrective discipline are two sides of the same coin. Each works best when they are held together. Parenting using only one side of the training coin is incomplete and deficient. So, what we want to highlight in this chapter is that corrective discipline requires a foundation of positive instruction. And where better to look than Proverbs?[8]

In Proverbs we learn that biblical discipline is both positive and negative, both instructive and corrective. It's unhealthy for children when parents lean primarily on negative correction instead of saturating their homes with positive instruction. The overarching atmosphere of our homes must be one of positive instruction, where the corrective discipline happens only for willful defiance. If our parenting is characterized more by negative, corrective discipline than by positive instruction, or if our children are more accustomed to hearing *no* rather than *yes*, then we need to evaluate our parental focus.

Prioritize Positive Instruction

When our girls were little, I (Juan) would come home from work, and we would play the "Stop and Go" game. I'd ask the girls to stand next to the wall, and I'd stand several feet away. When I said "Go," the girls began walking toward me. They couldn't run, or they'd have to return to the wall. When they heard me say, "stop," they had to stop immediately. The one who followed the directions and tagged me first was the winner. So, as soon as I said, "go," they walked as fast as their little legs could carry them. Even while walking, they were trying to guess when I would yell, "stop," so as not to be disqualified. It was a simple game, but it had a point. We had fun, of course, but more importantly, Jeanine and I were teaching the girls to listen to our voices and obey. While to the girls it was just a game, to us it was an example of positive instruction.

We've learned that parenting should be characterized by positive instruction. Our *no* should be heard against the backdrop of a thousand daily *yes*es. Put another way, our homes should be characterized by encouragement and instruction, not criticism and correction. This kind of positive discipline requires intentionality, patience, hard work, and, well, discipline—which is why we tend not to do it. When parents are characterized by repetitive negative speech and the constant threat of corrective discipline, they are likely driven more by a craving for their own comfort and convenience than by their child's well-being. But remember that the good news of Jesus Christ applies to us as well. If you've sinned against your children, confess your sins and seek to make things right. Our God is a God of new beginnings, and your children will welcome your honesty. Such humble repentance displays the gospel to your children.

Parental discipline should also be life-giving, that is, edifying. Far from being life-giving, discipline that is only corrective without prior positive instruction is discouraging. When Juan taught our girls to swim, he taught a specific skill and then had them practice it in the pool. For example, Juan asked them to touch their chins to their chests while simultaneously kicking their feet. When they did so, their bodies remained horizontal, and they were able to propel themselves to the side of the pool. We practiced this newly learned skill until they perfected it. We didn't just throw them in the water and say, "Come to the side of the pool," or, "No! That's wrong!" Not only would that have been irresponsible and dangerous, but it would also have been frustrating. Instead, we taught them the skill, explained what we expected, and then helped them practice the new skill. Each year they improved, until they found themselves winning races on a competitive swim team.

How might we establish a home that is marked by such encouragement and positive instruction? Let's use Proverbs as a guide. It's not the only portion of Scripture that is pertinent for parenting, but it provides a helpful framework. Solomon wrote his proverbs to instruct his sons in wisdom in order that they may walk on the path of righteousness (Proverbs 1:1–7). Solomon reminds us that parental instruction is not just about increasing our children's knowledge of Scripture. Learning God's Word, as we have argued, is foundational. It is the content of our instruction. But our aim is not just to have children who can recite memory verses. Our aim is to help guide our children on the right path, which is the path of righteousness (2:6–15). To do that, we must constantly highlight the difference between the two paths before each of us and remind our children where each path leads. The way of wisdom leads to life (12:28; 13:14), while the way of foolishness leads to death (14:12). Using Proverbs as a framework and other pertinent Scriptures to bolster our argument, let's consider a few principles of positive instruction.

Principle 1: Teach what appropriate behavior is.

Too often, parents get frustrated with their children because they behave poorly. But why would you expect your child to behave properly if you've never taught her what you expect, or if you are placing unrealistic expectations on your child due to age, developmental stage, or physical ability? Imagine you and your family are eating dinner with special guests. You've been planning this dinner for some time, and now you are eager to host your guests. Your one-year-old is sitting well in a high chair and eating all her food. Suddenly, however, she starts spitting out her food. As she does, her food lands on your special guest. At first, you're embarrassed, but quickly, you get frustrated. Your initial reaction may be to correct her. But here are some questions to consider. Have you taught her what is appropriate high chair or mealtime behavior? Is she simply being childish? Is she openly defiant? Or was the food too hot for her tongue? Too often we expect our children to guess what our expectations are or figure out on their own why they are being corrected. That's unfair to them.

How can the Bible help us set our expectations for our children? Throughout Proverbs, Solomon appeals to prior instruction: "My son, don't forget my teaching" (3:1). As a father, Solomon regularly taught his sons the way of wisdom. The Proverbs themselves are one of the means he used. Although he pleads with his sons to keep his commands, we're meant to understand that the source of his instruction is Scripture, "for they will bring you many days, a full life, and well-being" (3:2). Like we said in chapter 6, the Bible must be the foundation for our positive instruction. So ground your expectations of appropriate behavior in Scripture. We will frustrate our children when we expect more from them than God does. What God has revealed is sufficient to lead our children on the path of wisdom and teach them what is appropriate behavior. Take the Ten Commandments, for example. Exodus 20:12 says, "Honor your father and your mother." This is God's Word, and we should teach our children to honor their parents. But we must also explain what that looks like in your culture, in your home, at their age, and at their stage of development. How are children expected to honor parents in your culture? What are your expectations for your children in relation to this command? How much are they able to understand? What are they capable of doing? So teach them appropriate behavior in ways they can understand and follow. Provide clear, realistic, and grace-filled expectations. Help them understand what you expect. Then, expect that.

As an example, we spent the early years of our marriage and parenting in the South. Because of the expectations of the Southern culture, we taught our children to say, "Yes, sir; No, sir; Yes, ma'am; No, ma'am." We also asked them to refer to adults by their appropriate titles: Mr., Mrs., Dr., Rev. Where Jeanine grew up, that is how they honored adults and their parents.

Principle 2: Teach what inappropriate behavior is.

Just as we are to teach our children what appropriate behavior is, we must also teach them what is inappropriate. This principle is simply the flip side of the first. In fact, these first two principles go hand in hand. Take a two-year-old who has always been compliant. Suddenly, he bites you. Ouch! Because you are surprised, your immediate reaction may be to take him into another room and chastise him. But ask yourself: Have you taught him previously that biting others is inappropriate? If the answer is no, use this incident as a teaching moment. Place your hand gently on his mouth and firmly say, "No. We don't bite. That hurt, and it's wrong to hurt someone else." With younger children, all you may need to say is, "Don't bite. That's unkind and wrong." Parental authority is sufficient at that young stage. But the older your children are, the more you have to ground your instruction in God's Word. So, if your four-year-old bites her sister, you may want to add a biblical reason why biting is wrong—"But if you bite and devour one another, watch out, or you will be consumed by one another" (Galatians 5:15). To be sure, Paul is using this passage to speak about interpersonal conflict, not literal biting, but the point is the same. And with a four-year-old, that may be sufficient.

Of course, there are many passages that help us highlight both appropriate and inappropriate behavior. Consider how the apostle Paul regularly outlined sinful behavior as a warning to Christians: "Therefore, put to death what belongs to your earthly nature. . . . But now, put away all the following: anger, wrath, malice, slander, and filthy language from your mouth. Do not lie to one another, since you have put off the old self with its practices and have put on the new self" (Colossians 3:5, 8–10).

If we don't teach our children what to expect, we will frustrate them. We'll leave them constantly guessing what behavior is appropriate and what is not. Rather than frustrate them, let's take time to teach them what to expect, and then hold them to that standard. Once we establish a standard of expectations that are grounded in Scripture and are age-appropriate and developmentally appropriate, we may begin encouraging the good and discouraging the bad.

Principle 3: Encourage obedience by highlighting the blessings of obedience.

Note how Solomon appeals to his sons in Proverbs 3. He encourages obedience to God's Word ("my teaching . . . my commands") by pointing to the blessings of obedience—"for they will bring you many days, a full life, and well-being" (v. 2). Also, he reminds them that if they maintain loyalty and faithfulness in their relationships, "then you will find favor and high regard with God and people" (vv. 3–4).

What might this kind of encouragement look like for us? At one level, this positive instruction with the promise of blessing ("many days, a full life, and well-being," v. 2) should serve as the foundation of our instruction (see Proverbs 1:8–9; 2:2–5; 4:7–8). For our unbelieving children, we are holding before them the promise of blessing that is found in Christ alone. For our believing children, though, because they are in Christ, the blessings are theirs already as they experience the love of Christ in their relationship with him (2 Corinthians 5:14). And as they remain in Christ (John 15:4–5), they will grow in obedience as the Spirit produces his fruit in their lives (Galatians 5:19–24). So teach your children about our glorious, gracious God—our Father in heaven. Explain what he has revealed is proper behavior and what is not proper behavior. Emphasize the joys and blessings of obeying him. Of course, one of the great blessings of obedience is our own happiness (John 15:9–11). At another level, you may also encourage obedience by highlighting the blessings of obedience in the moment—God's glory and our own peace and joy (1 Samuel 15:22; Ephesians 6:3).

Highlighting the blessings of obedience is not a "spiritual" way of bribing your children. It's important that we understand this, because we don't want to find ourselves using bad parenting practices. So let us explain. When we went into new situations, we would have car training sessions. First, we stated our expectations, then we highlighted the blessings for obedience. We used blessing language often because Scripture uses it often. Look it up! I (Jeanine) took the girls everywhere with me: the store, the doctor's office, friends' homes. Where I went, they went. If the girls ever realized they outnumbered me (there were five of them and only one of me), there could have been a coup. Thankfully, they generally responded well to our instruction. But, in the car, as we arrived at our destination, I wouldn't simply tell them how to behave. I asked them questions so they could tell me what I expected of them. You might be amazed at what your children come up with concerning right behavior in certain situations. Giving them an opportunity to think through things on their own and verbalize them to you not only helps them remember but also helps them take ownership of their actions.

> "Girls, we are going into the grocery store to pick up some items. What are some rules for how we should behave?"
>
> One might say, "We shouldn't touch anything that's not ours."
>
> "That's right!" I would reply, encouraging her response. The simple guideline of not touching things that aren't yours will be helpful in many places such as other people's homes.
>
> Another might say, "Stay near Mommy." Or "Stay seated in the cart."
>
> "Great job, girls. I need you to be a blessing while we are in the store."

Take the time to allow them to think and answer. Don't just rush through these steps. That's it—nothing fancy. But what is the blessing of obedience? you might be wondering. The blessing was that they had food for another day because I could complete the grocery shopping. They had the blessing of a joyful mother, the blessing of a happy family, and my praise at the end of the shopping time. No candy, no toys, and no bribing. But there was a lot of praise: "Girls, you were such a blessing to me in the store! You made it easy to complete that task, and I am so thankful."

How does this work with older children or teenagers? We will flesh this out in later chapters, but when your teenagers are characterized by respectful obedience, they will be blessed with a joyful home and more age-appropriate freedoms.

Principle 4: Encourage obedience by pointing out the consequences of sin.

In Proverbs 3:27–35, Solomon encourages obedience by pointing out the consequences of sin. Note his appeals to his sons: "Don't envy a violent man or choose any of his ways; for the devious are detestable to the Lord, but he is a friend to the upright" (vv. 31–32). The Lord curses the house of the wicked but blesses the home of the righteous (v. 33). Also, "he mocks those who mock, but gives grace to the humble" (v. 34). And he honors the wise but dishonors fools (v. 35). By pointing out the consequences of disobedience, Solomon appeals to his sons to obey.

Of course, such instruction also includes highlighting the ultimate consequence of choosing sin: destruction. What might this look like?

My (Jeanine's) parents were in town for the holidays, and we had planned a day trip. Everyone was excited. Still, we had to spend prolonged time in the car together, and sometimes that can be tricky. One of the girls was disobeying and even threw a tantrum earlier that day, but we were hopeful she would calm down before we left! We set our expectations before leaving, and off we went! Our expectations weren't crazy, just simple car etiquette.

Be kind to your siblings. Respect their space. The first part of the trip went fine. Then—we have no idea what happened. We could sense conflict escalating in the back seat. Remember that we had eight people in our van. That's when I intervened: "Sister, please keep your hands to yourself. How should you treat your sister? That's right, you should be kind to her. Is what you're doing blessing her? No, it isn't." Well, that didn't work. She didn't care.

The next step was for me to point out the consequences of her sin. Out of the many consequences we could point to, we chose turning the car around and going home. If she couldn't practice self-control in the car, she would lose the privilege of a fun day trip. We knew her well enough to know the entire day would be miserable if she continued her disobedience. Would turning the van around affect the whole family? Absolutely. But we set the standard and outlined the consequence. She chose to continue in her disobedience, so we calmly let the family know that we would need to return home. Our disgruntled daughter continued in her tantrum. When we arrived at home, she quickly exited the car and ran to the top of her playhouse in the backyard. Was this the end? Absolutely not! While the rest of us went inside, Juan climbed up the small ladder and sat down with her in the playhouse. She didn't need a lecture. She wouldn't have listened. And she experienced the natural consequences of her actions—a canceled day trip of fun with family. Instead, Juan and our daughter had a conversation in which he asked her lots of questions to try to get to her heart. "Zoe, did your sin in the vehicle bring you a blessing? No, it didn't. Because you chose to disobey Daddy, we all lost the privilege of our family day. What could you have done differently?" Juan was trying to guide her to verbalize what she already knew. We had already explained our standard. We had taught her God's Word. She sinned. Sinners need a Savior. At this point you may be feeling sorry for Zoe, for our other girls, and my parents. Don't worry. My parents supported us. They understood that a child left to her own way will continue down the path that leads away from life and blessing.

In our house, we often used "If . . . Then" language. The girls knew the warning and the consequence beforehand. We even had an "If . . . Then" chart hanging on our wall! It would list the offense (*If* arguing, complaining), an appropriate Scripture reference (Philippians 2:14, "Do everything without grumbling and arguing . . ."), *then* the appropriate consequence (additional chores). As you can imagine, you can create your own chart with the attitudes and behaviors you want to address. Contrary to what you may think, "If . . . Then" language is not a threat. Instead, it encourages our children to obey by clearly pointing out the consequences of their sin. We help our children by establishing now that all sin and disobedience has consequences. This encouragement remains equally important for your older children or teenagers. When you say, "If you do not get your homework done this week and turned in on time, you will not have the freedom of going out with your friends," stick to it. You have given an expectation, a command, and a clear consequence. Stand firm to help them learn that all decisions, both good and bad, have consequences.

Shepherd Their Hearts

As we think about *how* to instruct our children, it's important to remind ourselves *why* we are instructing them. We're not doing it simply so we will have well-behaved children. The purpose, or the goal, of spiritual parenting is to reach their hearts! We want our children to obey from the heart! Solomon was a wise king and father, and he knew that true obedience flows from the heart. Notice his emphasis on the heart in Proverbs 3: "let your heart keep my commands" (v. 1), "write [loyalty and faithfulness] on the tablet of your heart (v. 3), "Trust in the Lord with all your heart" (v. 5). As we train our children from God's Word, we pray to see the fruit of heart obedience (vv. 8–11). Changed behavior is a glorious fruit of a changed heart. But new hearts are what our children need most. So instruct your children from God's Word, appealing for obedience by showing them the blessings of obedience and pointing out the curses for disobedience. And remind your believing children that they are not obeying to keep the blessing but out of a love for Christ. Jesus obeyed in their place and received the curses for their disobedience on the cross. As believers, then, our obedience is an act of worship. Because of God's mercies toward us in Christ, we offer our whole selves to God as a living sacrifice that pleases him (Romans 12:1–2). Don't stop praying that God would give your unbelieving child a new heart. And be sure to keep praying for your believing children to grow in the wisdom and knowledge of Christ. In fact, prayer is where we begin (see chapter 4). Much of our parenting happens on our knees.

A helpful way of understanding biblical parenting is as shepherding the heart. By our instruction, we are laying the foundation of God's Word and what God expects. God's commands reveal how we are to relate to him and to one another—in love (Romans 13:8–10). God's covenant promises reveal his character. He is "a compassionate and gracious God, slow to anger and abounding in faithful love and truth, maintaining faithful love to a thousand generations, forgiving iniquity, rebellion, and sin. But he will not leave the guilty unpunished, bringing the consequences of the fathers' iniquity on the children and grandchildren to the third and fourth generation" (Exodus 34:6–7). We are helping our children understand who God is and what he has done for us in Christ. Though they are sinners in need of new hearts, we are teaching them God's Word, God's commands. As they strive to obey, they will realize their inability. This allows us to point them to Christ and the promise of a new heart. And, like us, our believing children need to constantly be reminded of the gospel. As they strive to obey, we remind them they are accepted already before God because of Christ, but God delights in our obedience. We shepherd our children's hearts by positive instruction and then, in age-appropriate and developmentally appropriate ways, explain the gospel that empowers our obedience. Of course, when their response to God's Word and God's commands is one of rebellion and unrepentance, then we will need to practice loving, biblical, redemptive, age-appropriate, and developmentally appropriate corrective discipline when necessary—that too displays the gospel.

Practice Corrective Discipline

We wish that all we had to do was provide positive instruction, reminding our children of the blessings of obedience and the dangers of sin. But because we're all sinners, we need to be corrected. That includes our children. And God knows we need correction since he tells us in his Word that the Word is profitable, not only for teaching and training, but also for rebuking and correcting (2 Timothy 3:16). In fact, one of the ways God deals with us as sons is by disciplining us. It is our heavenly Father who establishes the motive (love), the purpose (to share in his holiness), and the fruit (righteousness) of corrective discipline (Hebrews 12:5–11).

Still, even when motivated by love and doing it for the right and godly reasons, applying corrective discipline requires wisdom. After all, each of our children is uniquely and wonderfully made by God. Each child responds differently to correction. Each of our children is at a different place of understanding, development, and physical and intellectual abilities. For example, our youngest daughter was naturally compliant and tenderhearted. A gentle rebuke was often enough to correct her. Her older sister had attention-deficit/hyperactivity disorder (ADHD). Because of how God uniquely and wonderfully made her, she seemed naturally rambunctious. She often required more than a simple verbal rebuke, and the discipline process could take a significant amount of time.

According to Scripture, corrective discipline is an act of love. And it must be done in love in order to point our children down the path that leads to righteousness and life. Again, Proverbs help us. Notice how Solomon warns his sons, "Do not despise the Lord's instruction, my son, and do not loathe his discipline" (Proverbs 3:11). When we practice both positive instruction and corrective discipline, we're following the example of our Father in heaven.

Also notice the reason Solomon gives his sons for not despising the Lord's instruction and discipline—"for the LORD disciplines the one he loves, just as a father disciplines the son in whom he delights" (3:12). To practice corrective discipline is to love your child.

The reverse is also true: to withhold discipline is to withhold love (13:24). Why? Because if we allow our children to raise themselves and do whatever they want, we are simply training them into selfishness and sinfulness. We are allowing them to run freely down the path that leads to destruction. When we discipline our children, though, we are warning them about the coming judgment on the Last Day. If children continue on the path of foolishness, they will fall into the hands of a holy God. It is much better to fall into our hands and be corrected now. So we will practice loving, corrective discipline, considering the uniqueness of each child, in the hope that they will respond appropriately, ultimately embracing Christ.

One more thing: before we talk about the principles of corrective discipline, we need to warn about its misuse. It is wrong to administer corrective discipline in anger or out of frustration. That's what leads to abuse. Remember that we discipline in love and in age-appropriate and developmentally appropriate ways. But also know that chastisement—what the Bible calls "the rod"—is not the only form of corrective discipline. Again, Proverbs shows us various levels of corrective discipline that progress from the gentle to the firm. Let's turn now to some forms of corrective discipline, beginning with the gentlest forms and moving to the more severe.[9]

Level 1: Gentle exhortation

An exhortation is an urgent appeal to do something. As Paul Wegner points out, exhortations differ from positive instruction in that they are more personal and solemn.[10] An exhortation may come in the form of advice or argument; it may be an emphatic word or warning. Of course, the more serious the disobedience, the more severe the correction. Initially, though, corrective discipline may begin with a gentle exhortation. Listen to Solomon's exhortations in Proverbs 1. He begins with a term of endearment: "My son." He is personal, serious, and urgent: "If sinners entice you, don't be persuaded. If they say—'Come with us! Let's set an ambush and kill someone. Let's attack some innocent person just for fun!' . . . my son, don't travel that road with them or set foot on their path, because their feet run toward evil, and they hurry to shed blood . . ." (vv. 10–11, 15–16). Through personal, solemn, urgent appeals, Solomon guides his sons away from the path that leads to destruction.

The gentle exhortation should be a regular tool in our parenting tool belt. Too often, we overreact. We are tempted to treat every disobedience at the same level of seriousness, which, then, requires the same level of severity in our response. But what if we regularly exhorted our children instead? What if, as we lived our lives, we pointed out the dangers of sin and appealed to our children to continue walking down the path that leads to life? Say your son comes home from school and tells you about an incident where a classmate got into trouble. You could take time to walk through that incident, asking clarifying questions. Then you could gently exhort your son, "My son, if people ask you to join them in cheating on a test, don't be persuaded. If they ask you to help them steal someone's money, don't follow them down that path, because you saw what happened to your classmate when he broke the rules. More importantly, God tells us in his Word, 'Do not steal' (Exodus 20:15). When you cheat on a test, you are stealing someone else's answers, that person's hard work and preparation. When you take someone's money, you are stealing a gift given by that person's parents. That person's parents worked hard for that. It doesn't belong to you. So, remember that if your friends or classmates ask you to join them in those things, don't do it." These conversations take time, but they are important. We should be having them regularly. However, there will be times when our children disobey, and in those cases, they need to be corrected.

Level 2: Gentle rebuke

Think of rebuke or reproof as a word of correction when your child does something wrong. It addresses a specific disobedience, and it too is given in love, "for the LORD *reproves* him whom he loves, as a father the son in whom he delights" (Proverbs 3:12 ESV, emphasis added). Wise children receive rebuke given in love and, in return, love those who correct them (Proverbs 9:8). Foolish children, on the other hand, reject rebuke (9:7–8; 15:12).

The purpose of a rebuke is not to say, "I told you so!" That never helps, and, in fact, it is often discouraging. We offer a rebuke so that the one needing correction may gain knowledge (19:25). So after your child disobeys, gently point out what he did wrong. If you've invested in positive instruction, remind him of your standard. Help him understand how he violated that standard. Then, after you've explained what he did wrong, correct him. Too often, parents point out the wrong without helping children see the way forward. For instance, just saying, "Don't touch," is not helpful. Instead, gently rebuke, saying something like, "this is a 'no touch.'" Then redirect the child and offer him something he can touch and play with and remind him, "This is a 'yes touch.'" The Bible provides a pattern of corrective discipline: identify the sin and point the sinner back in the right direction. This will be an ongoing practice. As your children grow in understanding, you too will need to grow in gently pointing out wrong behavior and redirecting them toward the right path. And when your child's sin is more serious, your rebuke may be more serious.

Level 3: Chastisement or corporal punishment that does not cause harm[11]

We realize there is controversy over corporal punishment or spanking. That's one reason we prefer the word *chastisement.* By using that word, we mean to distinguish what the world views as the misapplication and abuse of spanking from the biblical use of "the rod." Each parent will have to come to his or her own conclusions about this matter. When considering corporal punishment, we must take into account each child's uniqueness, age, capacity to understand, individual personality, and psychological makeup. We must also consider the societal laws, norms, and expectations in cultures where corporal punishment is wrongly equated with abuse and in cultures where corporal punishment is practiced in abusive ways. There are other ways to chastise your child besides spanking, and many parents will choose to use different consequences. Chastisement may take the form of verbal rebuke, as mentioned above. It may take the form of a time out or separation from other children. It may involve you taking your child who has lost self-control and holding him lovingly and firmly in your arms until he regains his composure. Or chastisement may involve using a combination of approaches. For example, if we were sitting on the couch reading aloud and one of the girls became defiant and required correction, our first response would likely have been to send her to our room to our "red chair." One of us would have said something like, "You've lost the privilege of reading aloud with us. You may be excused to go to our room and sit in the red chair. We want you to think about why you've been excused. When you've calmed down, let us know, and Mommy or Daddy will be back to talk." We would then go to our room and have the conversation we needed to have. Regardless of what form chastisement might take, the important thing is that consequences are applied.

As we see from Proverbs, though, *the rod* or corporal punishment is a biblical form of corrective discipline. In fact, Proverbs 13:24 reminds us that "The one who will not use the rod hates his son, but the one who loves him disciplines him diligently." Why use physical corrective discipline? It gives wisdom. "A rod of correction imparts wisdom, but a youth left to himself is a disgrace to his mother" (29:15). Loving, measured physical chastisement may save your child's life as it leads him away from the path of destruction (19:18).

Biblical physical chastisement, while clearly a negative consequence, is never meant to cause harm. An important principle that can serve as a guide to physical chastisement is the biblical principle that "the punishment must fit the crime." In Scripture, we know this principle as "an eye for an eye" (Leviticus 24:17–22). It's a principle of justice meant to protect the guilty from receiving a punishment greater than the crime that was committed. It was also meant to protect against revenge. This principle will serve as a helpful guide in parental discipline through all stages. It protects against abuse, and it also forces us to think carefully about how we administer discipline, especially in those cases when a parent decides that rebellious disobedience may call for physical chastisement.

So, why do you chastise? For clear defiance and rebellion, that is, direct disobedience. "Wisdom is found on the lips of the discerning, but a rod is for the back of the one who lacks sense" (Proverbs 10:13). You chastise foolishness, not childishness. That means you have to distinguish between the two. "Foolishness is bound to the heart of a youth; a rod of discipline will separate it from him" (Proverbs 22:15). Think of an example with us. Say your two-year-old is learning to sit in a booster chair at your dining room table. During the meal, he spills his milk. It gets all over you. What do you do? If we had spilled milk at our table as children, we'd likely be yelled at. On extreme occasions, we were belittled. But if the spill was an accident and not disobedience, then it is a result of a child's limitations. Why would you rebuke, much less chastise, for an accident? You wouldn't. Instead, you'd gently exhort the two-year-old. You'd help him understand that this is what happens when you don't pay attention. You may respond by giving him a sippy cup or moving the cup out of his reach. Whatever you do, you want to set him up for success.

On the other hand, if your four-year-old throws her glass of milk across the table at her sister in anger after you have told her to be kind and have self-control, that's an entirely different situation. In our home, that foolish act would call for removing her from the table and sending him to our bedroom—remember the red chair? She would wait there until she and I calmed down. Then, at the appropriate time, I would go into the room. We would talk about what happened. I'd ask her to identify what she did wrong. I would then encourage her to ask God for forgiveness because all sin is first and foremost against God. Then I would lead her to ask those at the table for forgiveness. Then we would model forgiveness by saying something like, "Of course, I forgive you. I love you. And our Father in heaven loves you. That's why he sent Jesus to die on the cross for our sins—because he would rather save us than punish us. So he punished our sin in his own Son." Then I would let her know calmly that even though he has confessed his sins and received forgiveness, sin still has consequences. After chastisement, I would hold her in my arms, and we would hug and pray. I would remind her I love her and guide her to ask everyone at the table to forgive her, beginning with her milk-soaked sister.

Chastisement must always be appropriate for the child's age, individual personality, intellectual development, and psychological makeup. And we can't stress this enough; it must be nonharmful. It may hurt, but it will not harm (Proverbs 23:13). During the process of chastisement, we also want to maintain the dignity of the child. That means we don't chastise in public or in front of the other child, and it means that when we do chastise, we maintain the child's modesty and dignity. Also, make sure your child understands why he is being chastised—have him verbalize it himself. Then explain that the discipline he is receiving now is a mercy, a way of keeping him from a destructive path. Finally, reconcile with your child, and embrace him to express your love for him when the discipline process is completed.

A word of caution: when we become frustrated or angry with our children, we may be tempted to yell or to turn immediately to physical punishment. If that's you, during those times, you may need a "time out" until you can maintain self-control. Yelling is not a biblical form of discipline. It is sinful, demeaning, and slowly chips away at a child's self-worth (Ephesians 4:29). Ask the Lord for grace and wisdom to fight your anger. Seek help from your pastors or a biblical counselor. And patiently use all means of nonphysical correction at your disposal. If you are characterized by anger, don't use physical forms of correction. In fact, don't correct immediately. Take some time for yourself and your child. Ask God to give you the grace you need to bless your child. And consider other ways you may correct your child. Ask someone to help you with your anger. A good question for all moms and dads to ask of someone else who knows them well would be, "Have you seen me discipline in anger?" Most of us are not good at identifying our anger problems. We're all sinners in need of grace, and, because of Jesus, we can come to the Father and find grace to help in our time of need (Hebrews 4:14–16).

Conclusion

Parenting is hard! It's the hardest thing we've ever done! So get help. Find older couples that you admire. Get to know people in your church whose children seek to honor and obey them. Ask them what they're doing. Ask them where they learned to parent. But know that what was helpful for them might not work for your family. It's naive to assume we will discipline each child the same way. The book of Proverbs gives us a wide array of applications of discipline so that our children may walk in wisdom! Prioritize positive instruction. Remember that your children were born sinners, rebellious by nature. Seek to lead your children to heart obedience. That will point your unbelieving children to their need for Christ, and it will remind your believing children that they can, in fact, obey, because they have a new heart and God's Spirit within them. And practice corrective discipline that is appropriate for each age and stage of intellectual development. We're parenting for the long haul, not just the moment. It may be hard now, but pray for your children, point them to Christ, and show consistent faithfulness, trusting God with all your heart for the results. And finally, I want to emphasize that you are not justified by your parenting; you are justified by grace alone through faith alone in Christ alone!

Talking Together

This chapter may have challenged your approach to corrective discipline. Maybe you've come under the conviction of the Holy Spirit because you've been too harsh or because you've been too lax. If you've been too harsh, we encourage you to confess your sin and ask your children to forgive you. If you struggle with anger, get help. Ask your pastors to help you. Maybe they can counsel you or help you find a counselor to help you address your anger issues. If you've been too lax in your discipline, you too will need to confess your sin and repent. You've been allowing your children to go their own way and have not pointed them on the right path. Our Lord is gracious and merciful. His grace is sufficient to heal family wounds and allow us a fresh start. Let's think about some ways we may all begin anew.

1. Are you characterized more by positive instruction or corrective discipline? Can you identify why? What are some steps you can take to begin practicing both together?
2. In what ways does understanding the different levels of corrective discipline help you shepherd your children's hearts toward the path that leads to life? Which level do you need to practice? Which level are you overusing?
3. What have you learned about chastisement from this chapter? How will you apply those lessons in your parenting?
4. Make a list of things you want to discuss with your spouse, loved one, friend, mentor, or study group after reading this chapter.

Chapter 8

Parenting and Discipline in the Younger Years (0–5 years)

Principle: If we are to raise our children in a manner that honors God, we must consistently apply biblical instruction and discipline wisely and lovingly according to each child's age, individual personality, intellectual abilities, and psychological makeup.

There's nothing quite as overwhelming and exhilarating as starting your parenting journey. No matter how the Lord blessed you with children, it's an adventure full of hopes and expectations. Do you remember when you brought your baby home from the hospital or received approval for your adoption proceedings? That was the point it hit you: "I'm going to be a parent!" And almost immediately, you also realized just how hard parenting was going to be. Babies don't sleep when they're supposed to. Feedings are not as easy as you thought they would be. In fact, there are days when nothing goes as planned. So you reach for the computer and search the internet for answers. You ask your friends or fellow church members for advice, and what do you hear? "You just have to get through it. You'll survive." Not very hopeful, is it? And the problem is that this "phase" never ends. That five-month-old wriggling off the changing table turns into the toddler throwing a tantrum, then the preschooler who doesn't want to drink juice out of the green cup, then the ten-year-old who rolls her eyes and huffs off in disgust. Then you wake up one day and wonder how you will ever get through the teenage years because your teenager never comes out of his room and avoids all family interactions.

Parenting is like building a house. The foundation is crucial, and so are the blueprints. There are important steps in building a firm foundation so that when you do hit the teenage years, prayerfully, they won't always be characterized by rebellion. That's why we've tried to carefully lay a biblical and theological foundation for parenting in chapters one and two. It's why we provided a general road map in chapter three for moving from a child-centered home to a parent-directed home. And having built a foundation in the early chapters, we provided the building blocks of faith-fueled prayer, parental example, and biblical instruction in chapters 4, 5, and 6. Of course, our children will also require corrective discipline, and we tried to encourage you to do that biblically in chapter 7.

Now it's time to apply these general principles in more specific age-appropriate and developmentally appropriate ways. So, in this chapter, we will consider parenting and discipline in the younger years; in chapter 9, the middle years; and in chapter 10, the older years. As you proceed through these three chapters, you'll see how, in each one, we are walking back through the important principles laid down earlier and applying them in ways that are appropriate for children in that age group. It bears repeating that we don't present ourselves as experts or as if we've somehow unlocked the secret of faithful parenting. We're here at this point in the book because, while many Christian parenting books are helpful and encouraging in grounding us in grace and the gospel, most of the questions we get from parents are about where the rubber meets the road—practical application of general principles. These are the same questions we had as we were raising our children. In the introduction, we asked you to imagine yourself at a coffee shop. Recall that picture to your mind now. We've come to meet with you. And now, we're just going to talk about our children—yours and ours. We'll talk about what we did, the mistakes we made, what we learned, and what might be helpful to you. We're glad you're here. Let's grab some coffee and chat for a bit. What's on your mind?

Laying the Biblical Foundation

Question: How may I begin laying a foundation of biblical instruction?

That's a great question and the right place to start. I remember Juan coming home from the office one day and sharing with me an encounter he had with a church member: "Bible, Bible, Bible! That's all you talk about!" That was the church member's complaint, and he was exactly right. Do you have a problem in your marriage? Let's see what the Bible says. Are you struggling with anger? Let's go to the Bible. If that's God's design for us as adults, to seek him first and his kingdom, that's also where we should be starting with our wee babies. If you feel inadequate for the task ahead of you because your Bible knowledge is in its early forms, be encouraged! You can learn right along with your children. Laying a biblical foundation should include the elements of reading, Scripture memorization, family devotions, prayer, and a love for God's church.

Reading

Reading is a basic skill for discipleship, and reading takes time. Some of our best family memories were around books—all kinds of books! We had board books in baskets around our house. One of our toddling daughters would try to carry that basket around, plop herself on the ground, and flip through the books. Books were an easily accessible item in our home. Even if you are in a place in life where you can't afford to buy a lot of books, we've found the local library to be a helpful resource. Not only did we have books around the house, but we also even had a basket in our vehicle so that the girls had access to books while we drove. Need entertainment? Have a book! Bored? Read a book to them! Your small children have such curious minds, so take advantage of that. The stories in the Bible are full of wonder and awe! And your children don't have to know how to read to enjoy books. Allow them to manipulate the books, look at the pictures, and, even pretend to read aloud as they make things up.

One important element in our evening routine was read-aloud time. You will hear us mention this repeatedly. It's something we still do even with young adult children at home. Read-aloud time in the evening as we lounged on the sofa was such a sweet family time. What do we mean by read-aloud? It really is as simple as it sounds: reading out loud to your children. In the early years, it starts with picture books while they sit in your lap. When they grow too big for your lap, they sit next to you. There were times when I had a child on my lap, one on each side, then another lounging over my shoulders on top of the sofa. Everyone wanted to see! When we started reading shorter chapter books, the girls would get out coloring books or quiet toys and play around the coffee table as we read aloud. This takes training, which we will discuss later in this chapter. One of our daughters reads chapter books to her children while they take a bath—redeem the time! We read books that brought us laughter and some that brought us tears. We read biographies, historical fiction, fantasy, and some that were just plain fun.

Read-aloud wasn't necessarily focused on Bible teaching. Still, it was a time that taught our children a love for reading and how to sit still for prolonged periods of time. These are important foundational principles for learning Scripture and growing in obedience. And frequently it's a time of learning while having fun. For example, many of the books we chose helped us teach our children how to treat people with kindness. One of our favorite books was *What If Everybody Did,* which talks about funny consequences of our actions. We could apply what we learned if kids wanted to pick a rose from the neighbors' bush. That may seem fine, but "what if everybody did?" They now had a category for their behavior using fun means. *Handy-Dandy Helpful Hal* helped us see the value of working hard and helping your family with chores. There are so many wonderful resources out there that can undergird your family values and teach them in a fun, engaging, and memorable way.

Scripture memorization

If I asked you how important Scripture memorization is, you would emphatically say it's very important! But we all have excuses as to why we don't do it. There is a wide variety of resources to help with Scripture memorization. Memorize Scripture to music, for example. If I asked you to sing a popular song from your teenage years, you could remember every single word. That's the power of music—the repetition of words put to catchy tunes helps you remember. During the girls' playtime, we had fun music playing in the background that reinforced our biblical values. We also listened to children's adventure shows like *Adventures in Odyssey* while riding in the car.[12] Each show highlighted Scripture principles and reinforced them through singing. So imagine a road trip where our family is singing about faithfulness, being a good friend, or putting Christ first. Then when a situation came up, we could sing the song as a gentle reminder to make a good decision. Music is such a powerful tool, both for good and for ill, so listen wisely!

You'll be surprised by what your children can memorize. I decided to redeem the time while changing my girls' diapers by reciting *A Catechism for Boys and Girls* with my infants. Catechisms teach doctrine in a systematic way through questions and answers. Their little minds will recall these truths as they grow and mature. We started with the first question and just moved along. This is "drop in the bucket," Deuteronomy 6-type teaching. Think of your child's mind as an empty bucket. As your child grows, someone or something will fill his or her mind. By our instruction, we are placing "drops" of God's wisdom into their little buckets, slowly filling it up. Wisely use every moment you have with your children. Don't just turn on the radio or television. Don't just hand them a screen, then check out. Put down your phone. Engage with your children. Be the one to fill the bucket.

Family devotions

Our family devotions during the early ages were primarily at bedtime. We would sit on the couch and read Bible story books, board books with biblical themes, then take the girls to bed, where we prayed and sang. Then, as they grew older, we often did family devotions at the meal table. Our kids were seated and were slow eaters, so we had a captive audience. We simply talked about the day ahead. I would read a small portion of Scripture, no more than a chapter. Then we went around asking how we could pray for one another. Normally, I would pray, then breakfast would be over. Because we made it a priority to eat together, this also helped us to be consistent. And we didn't take long because their attention span at this age was short. But each morning we wanted to add a drop in the bucket. Over years of consistent faithfulness, the bucket begins to fill. But don't think of Bible time in legalistic terms, where we *must* do this every night or at every meal, otherwise we are a failure. Or don't think that just because we did it at dinner, you must too. We had our family devotions when it was most convenient for us and when it ensured the greatest consistency. You need to find which time works best for you and your family. What time of day or night would offer the greatest opportunity for consistency?

Again, there is no magical formula for family devotions—just faithfulness. The key is to establish a time, find a place, and settle on a plan. If you can commit to those three acts, you're well on your way to consistent family devotions. During these early years, you are providing a framework for their understanding of the Bible and doctrines like God, sin, Christ, repentance, and faith. Think of their minds and hearts as the fertile soil for a future garden. You are planting seeds and watering them in an ordered and consistent manner, praying that the Lord, by his Spirit, will one day give them growth. Our aim is to be faithful gardeners, so that one day we might look upon that garden filled with beautiful flowers God blessed with life.

You are also preparing your children to face the influences of the world, the temptations of their own flesh, and the schemes of the devil. Satan wants your kids. The world wants your kids' hearts. And their own flesh (sinful human nature) seeks to lure them away through frustrated, unmet, and sinful desires. Raising children is not as simple as just protecting them from these things. You want to fill their minds with whatever is true, noble, right, pure, and godly (Philippians 4:8). This takes time and commitment and is crucial in raising godly offspring.

Admittedly, making time for Scripture reading, memorization, and devotions with your family takes time and sacrifice. For our family, we had to sacrifice our beloved television. During the week, we could either read or watch television. We didn't have time for both. Truth be told, this was a greater sacrifice for Juan, who used to watch news television on repeat! Stop and think, *What do I need to sacrifice to spend time reading and discipling my kids?* Then pray that the Lord would help you see the importance of laying a solid biblical foundation in this season. Laying this foundation will pay dividends in the following seasons of parenting!

The local church

We can't talk about laying a biblical foundation without talking about the church. Otherwise, our discipleship will be anemic. I know that at this age your children are only following you to church, but let me (Juan) say a word to you, Mom and Dad, about the role of the church in the life of the believer. It is vital at this early stage that you find a healthy church that preaches the gospel and provides a supportive community. And it will serve you well in the long run if you establish the rhythm of regularly gathering with God's people now rather than later.

Jesus speaks clearly in Scripture about the importance of the church, his body, for which he gave his life. But for too long, I had too small a view of the church. Then I read Ephesians carefully. There Paul explains that God's eternal plan is to exalt Jesus as King and Lord over all things in order to unite all things in him and submit all things to him. The Father has given this exalted Jesus to the church as its head (Ephesians 1:7–10, 19–23). The church is built on the foundation of the apostolic teaching, that is, the gospel of Jesus Christ (2:20–21). Through the preaching of the gospel, Jesus is gathering his multiethnic people (2:17–18). Through this same gospel, we build one another up in love until we grow to look more like Jesus (4:11–16). And as we live life together as a church, we display to the cosmic powers the wisdom of God's eternal plan in Christ (3:10–11). So the church is where Christians grow in Christlikeness. The church is where we learn to live as brothers and sisters in Christ. The church is where God displays the wisdom of all he is and has done for us in Christ.

How are you showing your family the importance of the local church in God's plan? Are you a member of a local church? Do you prioritize the weekly worship gathering? There is always something vying for your time and attention. Prioritize the local church. And don't let your children dictate where and how often you go to church. Raise your children in a church that preaches the gospel and teaches love for one another. We cannot love Jesus (the head) if we don't love the church (his body). And we want our children to love Jesus and his church.

What if your spouse doesn't go to church? That was my (Jeanine's) upbringing. My father wasn't a believer, but my mother was faithful. She woke us up and took us to church. Out of her faithfulness grew a love in me for our local body of believers. I looked forward to going weekly, then serving as a teenager. I rejoiced watching my mother develop deep friendships with the women there. I went to our pastor's home often and saw a healthy marriage modeled. This time my mother provided for me in my life was one of the most important things she did, and for that I am thankful. So, moms, be like Timothy's mother and grandmother and pass down a sincere love for God's Word and God's church.

Positive Instruction

After laying a biblical foundation, what parenting goals should we set for the early years? You might think sleeping through the night is of utmost importance. It is! How about having the self-control to not throw temper tantrums? This is also important. So are being kind to your siblings and not arguing with parents. We're sure you have your own list of parenting goals you'd like to work on.

Where to begin?

To the biblical foundation we add positive instruction. True religion, says James, is not just about hearing. It is also about doing (James 1:22–25). And our doing flows out of the heart—both the good and the bad (Mark 7:21–23). Since younger children will likely be unbelievers, their greatest need is a new heart that empowers obedience (Ezekiel 36:26–27). This reality should humble and encourage us. It humbles us because we cannot change our children's hearts. It encourages us because God can. This reality should also warn and correct us. It warns us to not be satisfied with mere obedience. Our ultimate goal is love for Christ. It corrects us from having burdensome expectations of our children and reminds us to be filled with grace.

Because our younger children are likely unbelievers, the role of positive instruction functions similarly to how the Law did in the life of Israel. The giving of the Law was an act of grace on God's part by which he communicated his expectations of and to his people. It was a standard that reflected his holiness. Because they needed new hearts, though, the Law also pointed to their inability to keep it in their own strength. That is, the Law pointed to the One who would come and keep the Law in their place—namely, Jesus. In the same way, we set biblical standards before our children—a standard that reflects God's holiness. Since Jesus has fulfilled the Law by his obedient life and sacrificial death, when we set a standard before our children, that standard is meant to point our children to the obedient Son who grants new hearts to all who believe in him.

Let's not lose sight of this glorious gospel. And don't underestimate the grace of God. He can and does save children at young ages. The Spirit blows where he wishes and grants life when God wills (John 3:8). Our positive instruction is meant to lead our children on the path that leads to life. This is why our diligence, intentionality, and consistency are so important. Positive training requires the mindset of training for a marathon, not a sprint. We are parenting for the long haul, not merely the moment. It requires the mundane thousands of daily steps of faithfulness. On hard days, you may feel like you can't go on. But remember that you have a goal in mind that's better than finishing a marathon, and it's worth it!

Teaching obedience

What is our goal in positive instruction? As God did with Israel, we are establishing the standard and communicating our expectation—obedience. And as God was toward Israel, we are to be "compassionate and gracious. . . slow to anger and abounding in faithful love and truth" (Exodus 34:6). This is another parenting tension, isn't it? We are to be full of grace and expect full obedience. As we learn from God's dealing with King Saul, incomplete obedience is full disobedience (1 Samuel 15). But the reason we must maintain a biblical standard, even if they will fail at it, is to point them to Jesus who has met it on our behalf. Our children's failure to meet God's standard reveals their need for Jesus. So look at teaching obedience as a necessary part of pointing our children to Jesus. And be careful to ground your expectations in Scripture, so as not to present an arbitrary standard, which may easily devolve into legalism. Having grounded your expectations in Scripture, maintain your standard.

As you are well aware, obedience doesn't magically happen. It takes not just one, but two methods to fully train your children in obedience. We must employ both positive training and corrective discipline. If you expect your little ones to know what obedience looks like while only disciplining for disobedience, they will be frustrated. Over the years, this frustration will chip away at a healthy parent-child relationship. We don't want that. We can head off some of that frustration through careful positive training. This training should have both a learning component and a time of practice. As you continue to practice the skill with consistency, you may need to add corrective discipline if your child is unresponsive. We'll talk more about what that looks like in the next chapter. So what does positive training look like? Where do you start? Consider with us some everyday opportunities to teach obedience with younger children.

No touch

I (Jeanine) was just at my daughter's house and was holding my almost one-year-old granddaughter, Leah. I had on an opal necklace on a thin silver chain, and its sparkle thrilled her. She eyed it and looked at me. Oh, how she wanted to touch it. Her mother had been training her in what we call "No touch." When Leah went to touch my necklace, I was able to gently redirect her hand and say, "Leah, that's a no touch." Her hand went down. Success! How did it happen? Her mother trained her to have self-control with her hands, and this training will be practiced for years to come. It starts with jewelry, the remote control, or your phone. These are not toys for little hands. Do you treat your cell phone as a toy? If so, it's an expensive toy, and when it gets broken, you'll likely be upset.

So how do we positively instruct for "no touch"? When your infant is old enough to sit in your lap, have some "forbidden fruit" nearby along with an age-appropriate toy. When they want to touch your glasses or your food on the table, you simply state, "That's a no touch, but this toy is a yes." You are saying no, but also providing a "yes." That's not just helpful, it's encouraging. When Adam and Eve were in the garden of Eden, God didn't place them in the midst of amazing trees and plants and say, "Don't touch anything!" He gave them a "Tree of No" in a "Garden of Yes" (Genesis 2:16–17). Of course, in their sin, they decided the one forbidden tree was better for them than all the freedoms in the garden. Since we have inherited Adam's sin and rebellion, your child will often make the same choice. We are, after all, like our father, Adam. For young children learning obedience and self-control, I cannot express how helpful it is to understand that the "no" exists in a garden filled with "yes!" It shows them that you are on their team, that you are their biggest cheerleader, and that you want them to succeed! If your child decides that obedience isn't the path they want to take in that instance, gentle correction reminds them that the forbidden fruit just isn't worth it.

One tool we learned to use to teach self-control was the folding of hands. We don't remember who told us about it or why it was so effective, but it was. Teaching your child to fold his hands when he is getting upset or about to lose self-control serves as a visual and physical example of self-control. We taught our kids this during times of nonconflict (positive instruction) beginning in the high chair when praying before a meal. At first, I had to hold their hands together, even when they didn't like it. From this training, when we encountered a "no touch," we simply asked them to fold their hands. And I, too, would fold my hands. You know that moment when your son is beginning a meltdown, when he is getting close to the edge of losing it? That's a perfect time to say, "Let's fold our hands, take a deep breath, and gain some self-control." If you teach this in a time of nonconflict, it becomes a helpful tool in your children's toolbox whenever they need to practice self-control.

Of course, during the early years, consistency is of utmost importance. Parent today how you want to live tomorrow. It's much easier to train correctly now than to retrain and undo misguided or bad habits later. Of course, the nature of parenting is that you will be doing both regularly—positive instruction and correction. Still, devoting yourself to positive instruction during the early years will go a long way to establishing that foundation you can return to time and again. So think of some simple, ordinary, and everyday ways you can teach your child obedience. The key is to practice correct behavior while correcting wrong behavior over and over until it becomes a new habit. Practice day in and day out for small increments of time, and you will be amazed at the small steps your child (and you!) will take toward obedience and self-control. This becomes more successful the more times you do it throughout the day, in different situations and locations throughout your house. Regularly choose a different place to practice "No Touch." You only need to practice for five minutes or less, then direct your child somewhere that's a Garden of Yes! Notice that, at this stage, I'm not quoting Scripture each time in our training. This stage takes minimal talking and a lot of action. This isn't where you provide a discourse and mini-sermon on 1 Corinthians 13 and how to love your neighbor. That comes later.

No whining or complaining

As your children learn to talk, their dissatisfaction with your standard may now be verbalized. You give a command and are met with a verbal noise that reminds you of a wounded animal. It's a natural gift all young children have, and sadly, we nurture it like a family pet. We stroke it by allowing it and giving into it. Then, suddenly, we find ourselves in a verbal struggle when we tire of it. We're talking about whining, of course. And its cousin, "complaining," is never far behind.

Admit it. We're all prone to whining and complaining. Still, it's like fingernails to a chalkboard when we hear it coming from someone else, especially our own children, and especially when it's directed at us. So we positively trained our children for self-control, because isn't that what whining and emotional outbursts are—lack of self-control? Whining is both a verbal and heart issue. It's verbal in that sometimes your kids just want to let you know something they need or want. It's a heart issue when they are not getting their way, and they are displeased. And what do we do? We often give in to it, therefore reaffirming the effectiveness of that means of communication. "I'm hungry!" or "I'm cold." "He's bothering me!" "She took my clothes!" We heard that one a lot. Did you know you can train your kids to not whine?!

You might state, "Please go get dressed for bed."

And their response is, "But Mommy! I'm tired!"

Then you respond, and they whine back. You go back and forth, caught in verbal ping-pong. The three-to-five-year age group is when whining and complaining becomes an art form. Whining is disobedience. And incomplete obedience is full disobedience.

When we tolerate whining and complaining, such disobedience is a parental issue and not just a child disobedience issue. By allowing whining and complaining, we are teaching them that that response is the way they will get what they want. So how can you train your children in a right response? By positive biblical instruction and negative corrective consequences. This three-to-five age range is when we started introducing references to Scripture. Philippians 2:14 is a verse that speaks well to this issue: "Do everything without grumbling and arguing." In our family, we also put whining into this category, because it's a heart issue similar to grumbling and arguing. Some Bible versions say "murmuring," "complaining," "questioning," or "hesitations." It's all the same.

How do we train for obedience without whining? First, don't model it. If we're not careful, we will teach our children how to do it. So seek God's help. Speak the truth to yourself. Don't whine or complain. Then remember that, just as you need God's help and God's truth, you are there to remind your children that those same resources are at their disposal. So don't tolerate whining and complaining. Don't listen to it. When the whine started oozing out of our child's mouth, I would stop her and say, "My ears can't hear you because you're whining. Talk to me in your big girl voice, and I will be able to hear you. Do you remember what Philippians 2:14 says? It says, 'Do everything without grumbling or arguing', and that includes whining. Let's gain some self-control. Fold your hands. Mommy will do it with you because I need God's help too to not whine. Now, let's try that again."

At times when your children's persistence continues, you may take them to a special waiting place. We had a reading chair in our bedroom. It was known as "the Red Chair." None of our children ever wanted to sit in it. Even today you can ask any of my girls about "the Red Chair," and many examples will come to their minds. When we needed our child to cool off, we'd say, "Let's go to the Red Chair." When we needed one of them to find self-control? It was, "Go to the Red Chair." I'd often say, "Wait in the Red Chair, and when you have found your self-control and can speak to me correctly, you may come talk to me." Because this chair lived in our bedroom, it was away from public view and attention. Why was it important for this chair to be away from the rest of the family? Because, at all times, we wanted to maintain each child's dignity, even in front of their siblings.

Think of helpful, creative, and gracious ways you can stop the flow of whining and complaining. Give your child the opportunity to gain self-control. Instruct on the right way to express your thoughts and feelings. And help them express themselves using helpful, honoring words. Consistency is key. After doing really well in staying on top of our kids both in training and correction, we often found ourselves loosening up a bit. This would lead to a need to reteach the same disciplines. It's always much easier to train and maintain good habits before bad habits take root than to retrain when that little weed has grown into a deeply rooted tree.

Utilize the family meal table

Another ordinary, everyday opportunity for positive instruction is during meals. Years ago we were out to lunch with another family whose children were younger than ours. We were thankful to be able to spend time with our friends and enjoy a meal together, but that's not what happened. Instead, the parents took turns watching their toddler and preschooler run around the restaurant because the kids were done eating. The children had not been trained to sit. Learning to sit is right up there with "no touch." And one of the most fruitful times of positive instruction can be around the meal table.

We sought to train our children to sit at the meal table—even after they were done eating. The meal table is a great place to learn self-control! When I cooked dinner, I'd often put a crawler or toddler in her highchair to contain her. I gave her a toy or a healthy snack. During snack time, which happened mid-morning and after nap, our children also sat at the table or in the high chair. When they could sit still in a high chair consistently, they graduated to a booster chair. And when they could sit politely in a booster on their bottom, they graduated to a real chair, sitting politely with their legs in front of them. We emphasized sitting on their bottoms because they struggled with self-control when on their knees. They couldn't sit still, going up and down. The chair became a gymnastics platform. We wanted our children to learn that an adult chair was a privilege that was theirs when they learned to sit "like a big girl." Again, though, we provided a Garden of Yes, even at the meal table. When our kids were done eating, we engaged in conversation. If they were too young to respond, we provided magnetic puzzle books nearby, or some other appropriate book, which had been set aside only for mealtime.

Most importantly, sitting together at mealtime allowed us to build relationships with our girls. In fact, it was a vital place where our family identity was developed and nourished. When our girls ate breakfast, we sat with them. At lunch time, I (Jeanine) was there. We prioritized eating dinner together. We learned that consistent parental presence encourages right behavior and builds relationships. For our family, the meal table, especially at breakfast, became the place for family devotions, family prayer, learning about one another's needs and concerns for the coming day, and cheering on our girls. My and Juan's regular mantra was, "We're your number one fan!"

Teach basic sign language

For children who have not developed verbal communication skills, we learned that sign language was a valuable tool. Words are not the only means of communication. And much to our surprise, we learned that our girls were communicating with us even before they could talk. In fact, our youngest didn't talk for the longest time, because she had four sisters who did all the talking for her. We learned that by introducing a few simple signs like "drink," "more," and "all done," we avoided whining, tantrums, or throwing food at meals. We saw that by teaching them to sign, "I'm sorry," we could work through forgiveness. And we took advantage of basic sign language to teach good manners, teaching them to sign "please," "thank you," "mommy," "daddy." These signs became useful for us even once we had verbal communicators. You try it. Teach your child basic sign language for "Please," "Thank you," "All done," "More," "Enough," "Drink," "Mommy," and "Daddy." All these signs and more allow your child to communicate with you rather than just getting frustrated because no one knows what he needs or wants.

Require eye contact and a verbal response

Before ending our discussion on positive training, we need to talk about verbal communication. Have you ever had a conversation with your kids, given them a command, and their eyes are looking all around the room? They leave your presence and forget what you asked them to do. Of course, you'd be frustrated. In seeking to fight against our own sinful frustration, we learned a few guidelines for how to give instructions and commands to our children. Require eye contact and a verbal response. At times, I had to help my kids put their hands up on the sides of their faces, like blinders on a horse, to help them focus. When I said, "I need you to focus," they knew to put their hands up. Just like holding hands to practice self-control, this small physical act allowed our children to focus on what we were saying. We also learned to ask them to repeat to us what we were asking of them. This small act assured us we were not misunderstood. So for example, when I gave the command, "I need you to go clean up your room," I often asked them to repeat the command back to me while looking me in the eyes. Some children needed to repeat the command aloud all the way up the stairs so they wouldn't forget. "I need to go clean up my room. I need to go clean up my room." That's how we knew they heard me and took ownership—when they repeated it back to me. If I didn't require them to repeat the instructions, I required a simple "Yes, Mommy/Daddy" or "Yes, ma'am/sir"—either verbally or in sign language. Eye contact and a verbal or sign response are key for clear communication.

Training your children at home makes them a blessing to you. It will allow them to be a blessing to others when you leave your house. When you are tempted to allow questionable behavior in your home, ask yourself, "What fruit will this bring somewhere else? Will this behavior bless others?" And if not, stop and train. Admittedly, though, training our children will sometimes require correction. But before we consider correction during the younger years, let's talk about some parenting traps to avoid.

Parenting Traps

By parenting traps, we're talking about bad habits or practices we fall into that give our authority away and strengthen our child's will. Remember that faithful parenting is about taking thousands of daily steps of faithfulness. It's not about heroics. It's about taking advantage of the everyday. And that's one reason parenting is exhausting. During the younger years, especially, you are always on duty. It is this overwhelming reality that can lead us to give in to our child's persistence. But we are not parenting in our own strength. At least, we shouldn't be. We parent in the strength of the Lord, in the power of the Spirit, in the confidence that comes from faith, and in gospel community—spouse, trusted friends, family, and the church. So, if you see yourself falling into these traps, ask for help, first from the Lord, then from your loved ones, and also from your church.

Giving too many freedoms

It's easy to fall into the trap of allowing your child to make his or her own choices. But remember the rectangle from chapter three. During the younger years, we need to exercise the most parental direction. The time for freedom will come as your child matures and consistently shows responsibility. The younger years are a time when children need to learn to come under your authority in a positive way. Your children will learn self-control by submitting to parental authority. This submission will serve them well their entire lives.

When do many parents begin to surrender their God-given parental authority? We realized that it all starts with clothes, sippy cups, and food. Have you ever found yourself asking your children what they'd like to wear, drink, or eat? "Do you want beans with your rice? Or would you rather have macaroni and cheese?" "Don't you want to come to Mommy so she can change your diaper?" "Do you want to wear your blue dress or your green one?" "Would you like to watch a show before bed?" "Don't you think it's time to go to bed?" If you haven't noticed it before, maybe reading the questions on paper makes the role reversal obvious. Someone is in charge in this relationship, and it's not the parent. If you are constantly directing your younger child through questions, you are slowly giving away your parental authority, and you're strengthening their will. State what you'd like them to do. Tell them, "It's time for dinner," "This is what is on the menu today," "It's time to get ready for bed." Remember that you're the parent. As your children mature and willingly obey, you will reward them with plenty of choices. In this way, they are learning that freedoms come with responsibility.

Excusing sinful behavior

Another way we give away our authority and strengthen our children's wills is by excusing sinful behavior. It's tempting for young parents to make excuses for their child's (or children's) sin. "They are tired." They're just hungry." "He's not used to this environment." The excuses are endless. Kids are smart! They will catch on that you're excusing their behavior, and they will take advantage of it. Excusing sin is not only wrong, but it will also make it harder for your children to obey in the long run. One question I used to ask myself is, "What will this behavior look like when they are ten or fifteen?" The whining over a meal grows into the ungrateful, entitled attitude of a teenager. Certainly, we need to learn to distinguish between childishness and foolishness. We also need to be students of our children so we may know their limits and capacities. We want to always be gracious and understanding with our children, but we don't want to excuse sin.

Being inconsistent

While inconsistent parenting may strengthen your child's will, more than likely, it will also prove frustrating to both parent and child. When your rules change depending on your mood or the time of the day, your child will get confused and, likely, become insecure. But, as a matter of self-preservation, some children may actually become hardened, since they don't know what to expect. They wonder, *Is this the nice Mommy today, or is she in a bad mood?* Failure to follow through on "no" is one of the most common inconsistencies in early parenting. We say "no," but tiredness and frustration make us want to give up the fight. If you don't say what you mean and mean what you say, you'll leave your children to wonder if they really have to obey. When we tolerate small acts of disobedience, they grow into a garden of defiance. Establishing consistent boundaries with clear consequences provides security and produces joy. Children will learn that every time they disobey, they will receive instruction or correction. They will realize they are not left to themselves. This breeds confidence in you and your authority.

Reasoning with young children

We want our children to think well and to make good choices, but they're not developmentally capable, at this stage, of abstract reasoning. They can handle only concrete ideas. That's why this stage is good for memorization and learning basic facts. So, when we try to reason with them to get them to obey, we're asking them to do something they're not generally equipped to do. I (Juan) remember having a two-year-old with me as I was walking into a bookstore while in seminary. She froze as we came to the entrance, so I thought I'd reason with her, explaining to her the reasons it was so important to obey Daddy and how doing so would bless her. As I was interacting with my daughter, I noticed two moms looking on with a smirk. That's when I realized, *It's OK to explain expectations at times, and at others, it's OK to simply pick up the child and go into the bookstore.* As they get older, they'll be able to embrace concepts like "but" or "why." In fact, early on, "why" will be a constant question. Their little minds are working. In those instances, give age-appropriate answers. Help them to develop their reasoning skills. But you're the parent. And during this stage, they need to learn obedience.

Bribing your children

Please don't bribe your kids to behave. Don't promise them a treat if they behave at the store. Don't promise them dessert if they sit still during dinner at a restaurant. Offering bribes for obedience will breed diminishing returns. And the law of diminishing returns reminds us that the more you bribe, the greater the bribe must become to appease your child. Additionally, you will teach them that they don't have to obey unless they're rewarded. But when your children learn to obey out of a love for you and a trust in your authority, you are free to express your love for them with gifts that are reflective of grace, not works. Bribes communicate that obedience is transactional: "If I do this, I get that." And that's the opposite of grace.

Threatening and repeating

You've seen that threatening, repeating parent. You've been that threatening, repeating parent. How do we know? Because we've been that threatening, repeating parent. How many times do you have to ask your child to complete a task? Does she do it the first time you ask? The second? The third? The fourth? If you find that it takes numerous times for your children to listen and obey, it's likely they've grown accustomed to your repeated threats. I guarantee you they know exactly how many times you will say something before you get serious. And because kids are smart, they know when you're serious. Of course, that's when they will obey. We taught our girls, "To delay is to disobey." To help them, though, we had to learn to say what we mean and mean what we say.

All these parenting traps undermine your parental authority. They frustrate our children and are likely to provoke them to anger and lead to insecurity. So train your child to obey through positive instruction. Expect obedience. Be consistent. And when your children still disobey, employ corrective discipline.

When Positive Instruction Transitions into Corrective Discipline

Even when you have trained your child and laid the foundation of positive instruction, you will still find yourself dealing with the same issues repeatedly. Therefore, as important as positive instruction is, don't be reluctant to employ corrective discipline. Let's review those three levels of corrective discipline we learned in chapter seven: beginning with exhortation, continuing with rebuke, and ending with chastisement. We've already addressed chastisement sufficiently in chapter 7, so here we will only review the first two levels of corrective discipline to make application for the younger years. But don't treat this as a formula. Remember that your child is fearfully and wonderfully (uniquely) made by God. So consider your child's age, personality, intellectual development, and psychological makeup. And don't worry! God has given you the wisdom to shepherd your unique child. How do I know that? Because along with the gift of his Son, God has promised to give us everything we need for life and godliness (Romans 8:32; 2 Peter 1:3). We're just here to help and encourage you. So if you need to, look over chapter 7 where we defined exhortation and rebuke. It's okay. We'll wait until you're ready.

Exhortation

As you walk to the changing table, for example, state your expectations. "Hosea, when I change your diaper, I want you to stay still." I know your six-month-old doesn't understand that, but you're building the foundation with positive instruction. Down he goes on the surface. He starts to wiggle, and you give him a toy. "Here's a toy you can play with while I change your diaper." Be firm, yet gracious. I often use an animated and fun voice to keep them engaged while training them. "No, Hosea. We're going to be still while I change your diaper." If he continues to wriggle away, you may need to gently correct that cute, pudgy, and little bundle of joy. There may be tears when he moves one way, and you firmly make him stay flat. My goal here was to train my child to lie still while I changed the diaper, and if necessary, exhort him gently. The key is consistency. Every time you change your child's diaper, you require obedience. Notice that it started with positive instruction, but because that wasn't heeded, it moved to corrective discipline. Giving a firm command with a warning, which should include a change in tone of voice, is level one of corrective discipline: exhortation. Firmness and anger are not synonymous. Firmness demonstrates significance, while sinful anger is heated and self-focused. Your children should notice that the fun-loving Mommy has been replaced by the serious one. This is one of your first instances of training toward self-control. As you consistently exhort your child gently, your child will learn. But there will be times when we will need to move to the second level of corrective discipline.

Rebuke

The rebuke is where you have exhorted and need to make the correction. Understanding the difference between childishness and foolishness is important. When they directly defy you, that is foolishness. When they make a mistake, or they are caught up in the moment of roughhousing and break something, that's childishness.

Childish hearts are not malicious or rebellious. Childishness is best dealt with by natural or logical consequences. Say your toddler purposely throws his toys off the highchair repeatedly. What's the consequence? He doesn't get them back. The behavior still needs to be corrected, but the correction comes from natural consequences. What if your child doesn't use a toy correctly after being told to be careful with it, and it breaks? You don't replace that toy. That's the natural consequence. Childish decisions abound in this stage. They still require correction, but you should allow the logical and natural consequences to be their teacher.

When our girls were younger, they loved taking their shoes off in the car. Because they could not yet tie their shoes, and because I thought Velcro tennis shoes were ugly, I had to put their shoes back on and tie each pair. . . every time we got out of the van. I realized I had to not only train them, but I also had to exhort them, rebuke them, and encourage obedience with a natural consequence. So I let them know when I put them in the car and buckled them in their car seats that they were not allowed to take off their shoes, and that if they did, I was not going to put them back on. All it took was taking a few steps on the cold driveway to realize the reason we wear shoes. That was an effective natural consequence.

Here's an important point to remember: when you exhort your kids and warn them of the consequences, they are making the choice themselves to embrace those consequences. It's not a surprise. They chose it. You aren't a mean parent, even though they may tell you that. And you don't even have to get upset about it. It's simple. My girls chose that day to walk the short distance from the driveway into the house in their bare feet on the freezing ice and snow. They learned a lesson that day—that disobedience is painful—and oh, how important that lesson is.

Logical consequences are a little different from natural consequences. A natural consequence is a, well, natural result of disobedience. A logical consequence is one you choose that is directly tied to the disobedience. For example, say your children are fighting over a toy. You need to correct them both. A logical consequence would be a loss of certain freedoms. The consequence that may make the most sense is that they can no longer play together. You may even want to sit them down in separate places until they decide they can play together. Maybe your child complains because she doesn't like the show you chose for her. What's a logical consequence? She loses the freedom of watching the show. You may wonder, what's the danger of allowing her to pick her show at this age? None really, if it's a show you have already approved for your household. Clearly, you would step in if your child chose a show that was inappropriate for their age. But some children are never satisfied, even with the show they choose. They're like four-year-old channel surfers. Again, you must constantly be on the lookout for heart attitudes. When your child can't choose her show and insists on having her own way, you may find that a rebuke, followed by logical consequences, is a very effective tool in rooting out childish behavior.

Conclusion

There was a study done where two groups of preschool children were taken to playgrounds to play.[13] One playground was surrounded by a fence, and the other was not. Interestingly, because the fence provided a safe barrier identifying the boundaries of the playground, the children felt free to utilize the entire playground space to play and explore. Ironically, the children at the playground with no fence congregated around their teacher and were more reluctant to play. That's a helpful analogy for what we're trying to communicate. Establishing biblical boundaries in the home provides a safe environment for our children to grow, develop, and explore. The point is that, rather than stifling our children, positive instruction and corrective discipline allow our children to feel safe in a loving environment where they may flourish and grow in wisdom and stature and, we pray, in favor with God.

Talking Together

The early years are foundational years. If you're reading this book and are in this stage, we want to help you build a strong foundation for the years to come. Enjoying the teen years begins now by laying a proper foundation. Let's think together about positive training and corrective discipline:

1. What are your biggest takeaways after reading this chapter? What are you doing well? What do you need to improve? What do you need to begin?
2. What are some ways you are using positive instruction with your children already? After reading this chapter, what are there some ways you can be more intentional in instructing your children?
3. How are you taking advantage of mealtimes at home? How do you need to change mealtime to redeem this opportunity?
4. How would you describe your current approach to corrective discipline in your home? How would you evaluate it? Has it been helpful and fruitful, or harmful and frustrating?
5. Did you recognize yourself in any of the parenting traps? If so, which one(s)? What can you do to avoid these traps?
6. Take time to talk with your spouse about your current practice of corrective discipline. Evaluate it together. Establish a plan moving forward. If you are a single parent, talk it over with a trusted friend or other Christian parents. If you are discussing these matters in a small group, try to learn from one another without judging those who are doing things differently.

Chapter 9

Parenting in the Middle Years (6–12 years)

Principle: During the middle years, we want to help our children understand why they must obey and begin taking ownership for their actions.

The middle years are such a tricky time. If your children are in the habit of telling the silliest knock-knock jokes you've ever heard, they are in this middle phase. If they've decided bathing and personal hygiene are optional, they are in this phase. If they argue with you like a graduate of Harvard Law School, they've arrived in and are slowly passing through the middle years. And as your children get older, they enter a stage often marked by sass and attitude, the rolling of the eyes, difficulty with relationships, and an overall pushing back on boundaries. At that point, they are trying to buck authority. And don't forget the hormones. As your children enter puberty, any given day is either the best day of their lives or the worst day ever. I wish I had a dollar for every time I heard that one! Sometimes there's no in-between, and they are probably just as frustrated as you are.

If you have not laid the foundation of expecting obedience, go back to chapter 7 and review those principles from Proverbs. Ask God to give you wisdom in knowing how and where to start. Start small. Choose one thing. Then slowly implement other principles one by one. And don't get discouraged. When I (Juan) realized I had neglected my responsibilities to be engaged in the instruction of our children, our oldest was six years old. I have to admit, doubts raced through my mind. "Did I wait too long? Were the first six years of her life lost?" And, of course, the answer was no, but those are the lies Satan wants us to believe and we're tempted to listen to. So wherever you find yourself in this parenting journey, you are here by God's providence, and you are not alone. You have Christ, his Spirit, his Word, and his church.

Maintain the Biblical Foundations

Life gets busier as our kids get older. We are encouraging their involvement in more and more extracurricular activities. But remember that the more things we say "yes" to, the less time we have for other important items at home. During this busy season, don't allow your extracurricular calendar to undermine the foundation you've already laid. If you only recently realized the need to establish biblical foundations in your home, don't worry.

Family devotions

As your children grow and mature, so should the content of biblical instruction. Of course, the foundational source of biblical instruction is Scripture. But you will also want to add tools that help you and your children understand Scripture. Regardless, be consistent. In our home, we were able to find small amounts of time to read the Bible and other books on doctrine that were age appropriate and not discouraging to their intellectual abilities. When you introduce children to material that is hard to understand, they will grow frustrated. This will work against your goals. So make this time enjoyable and stimulating. Allow your children to ask questions. They will ask many. And answer their questions honestly, but appropriately, regularly pointing them back to Scripture. And if you don't know the answer to one of their questions, admit it. Tell them that you too are growing in knowing Jesus and that it will be good for you both to learn together. This consistent practice will teach them to look to God's Word to find answers to life's hardest questions.

We also made sure to pray together. It encouraged us to hear our children's concerns. At this stage, their concerns may seem trivial to you, but they are significant to them. And if something was important to them, it became important to us. During this stage, they will also understand answered prayer. So share your concerns in appropriate ways. Invite them to pray with you. And celebrate when God answers your prayers. They will marvel at the God who hears them and answers their prayers. And when you pray for your children, pray encouraging prayers. What I mean is that you shouldn't use your time of prayer to lecture or preach to your children, like this: "O Lord, please make Becky obey today. You know how hard it is for her to listen to her parents." You pray like that in front of your children enough, and you will lose their hearts. Use family devotions to build relationships with one another. Make it a positive time, not a time to point out specific sins. Ask questions and encourage discussion. Show your children the beauty and riches of Christ and his Word!

Yes, there were times when our children didn't want to participate in family devotions. We didn't require them to contribute, only to listen. But their presence was never optional. Day after day and year after year, the Lord used those times to fill their hearts and minds with his truth.

Reading

As your children learn to read, their world expands! Also, as they become readers, they will be able to begin taking ownership of their own spiritual development. There are so many wonderful Bibles and books for young readers that will help them grow and learn about God. Since most children don't want to go to bed, allowing them to read at this time can be of great benefit. It's something our adult daughters living at home still do. This helps encourage them in their own personal devotions.

But, even at this stage, we continued to make time to read aloud with our children. Working through historical fiction gave us opportunities for rich discussions on topics we might not encounter in everyday life. We enjoyed biographies of people who inspired us to be whole-hearted followers of Christ. Reading aloud provided another time to positively instruct in what the Bible had to say about various issues. But not every book was a teaching time. It's important to enjoy reading just for fun. Because we lived in a big city and a lot of time was spent in a car, we even took books with us to read aloud on our drives! When I learned that my teenage girls were reading a book as they drove together in the car, it gave me such joy—they had developed a love of rich literature and stories from what we had done together as a family. Most mealtimes also had a component of reading aloud. In the evenings, instead of spending hours in front of a television, we read. It's what we did, and it bonded us together. Redeem the time; get creative! But remember that we don't just learn from one another at home.

The local church

An important part of their Bible instruction is a continued dedication to your local church. Children in their middle years may find church boring. They may prefer to do other activities. Your children may even get to a phase where they do not connect relationally with the kids their age at church. As a parent, it's important that you listen to their concerns and help them learn to problem solve. Each one of our girls went through this phase, and it was a chance for us to connect with them, hear their fears, and yet also help them learn how to reach out to others who might feel the same way. Encourage your children to develop relationships with other kids by pursuing time with families in the same stage as yours. You are developing an important habit as a family—Sundays are for worshipping with God's people, and this is a priority. It's also an important time when they are hearing God's truth from someone other than you. And after church you can help your children process what they heard and learned in their class or in the sermon.

Education choices

At this stage, you are making decisions about your child's education. Your child's education is a weighty matter, so don't make this decision lightly. Seek wise counsel. But whether you choose private, public, or home school, remember that you are your child's primary discipler. Don't assume that because your children are in a private Christian academy, they are receiving the needed biblical instruction. Don't think that because you homeschool your children, they are being discipled. Discipleship requires intentionality, and it requires relationship. No matter where your children go to school, you need to be involved in their education and in their life. Ask them what they are learning in school. Participate with them in their projects. Don't make them feel like a bother when they ask for help, because we are modeling how our heavenly Father desires for us to run to him for help in all things! Use science, math, history, and literature to teach them the wisdom of God, for all truth is God's truth. And pray! The wisdom from above is yours for the asking—that's what we see in Scripture.

From this stage forward, you should always be assessing the educational choices you have made for your children. If it seems that there's a clash between your school choices and your goal of raising your children according to God's desire, pray for clarity from the Lord. Proverbs 2:6 reminds us, "For the Lord gives wisdom; from his mouth come knowledge and understanding." Oh, how we need this wisdom, this knowledge and understanding, as we make choices concerning the long years of education for our children.

First-Time Obedience: Positive Instruction

What should obedience look like at this stage? When you tell your children to unload the dishwasher, they respond respectfully and complete the task right away and completely. When you tell them to go sit at the table and complete their homework, they do it. They don't argue with you and say, "But, Mom, I'm going to play outside for thirty minutes and then do it after dinner." That would be stealing your authority. When your kids learn to obey authority, and your authority specifically, it helps them have the self-control to deny themselves later in life.

Each stage of positive training should build on the foundation from the stage before. But how do you regain authority and respect if you haven't established it because you have not expected obedience? I mention respect because if they truly respected and trusted you, then they would fully obey you. Here is the most important way to do that: remind your children that you too are learning to obey Jesus and that you've realized you've been too permissive. Let them know you've asked God to forgive you and give you wisdom in how to reflect God's good authority in your home. Then ask them to forgive you and to pray for you. Talk about the standard you hope to set. And ask your children to help hold you accountable. You may only be beginning to establish a biblical standard in your home, or, like us at times, you may have gotten lazy and let your standard relax for a while. We found ourselves going through cycles when we had to ask for forgiveness, repent, and remind the girls of God's standard: faithful obedience. Remember: incomplete obedience is full disobedience. That became our mantra—something we had them repeat over and over again. As you reestablish the standard in your home, take time to teach and remind your children of your expectations. Explain the consequences for disobedience. And use every opportunity to emphasize faithful obedience. In our family, chore time was one of those teaching opportunities at this stage. Chores included making their beds and tidying their rooms before breakfast. We even provided a chart to remind them of their chores. This chart allowed them to take ownership of their obligations. Our aim was to set them up for success. We are always for our children, never against them. And to ensure the chores were done to our satisfaction, we inspected their work. If their work didn't meet our standard, they had to do it again. We'd help them at first, of course. But once we knew they could complete their chores on their own, that was our expectation. We equipped them, we outlined our expectations, and we communicated clear consequences.

When you have told your children what you expect of them, and they know the consequences, they make the choice to obey or disobey. They may choose the negative consequences if they don't think you'll follow through. Or they may just decide it's worth the gamble. So follow through. Mean what you say and say what you mean. Be consistent. Continually ask yourself, "What will this behavior look like as an adult? What fruit will this decision bring?" Otherwise, you will give your authority away and strengthen your child's will.

Clear, firm, and benevolent leadership seeks the well-being of those under its care. As parents, we not only want our child's temporal well-being, but we also want their eternal well-being. We don't sacrifice our standard to try and win our children's friendship or affection. That doesn't work. If we are inconsistent, we will lose both. You are the parent. Your children will have to choose how they will respond to your leadership. So make sure your leadership is worth following.

Getting to the Heart

We can't change our children's hearts, but God uses our daily, consistent, purposeful biblical instruction to bring it about. And the Bible has a lot to say about our hearts—the importance of searching our hearts and knowing their ways (Proverbs 4:23; Psalm 139:23–24). Much of the exhortation and rebuke that happens at this stage involves getting to your child's heart! This is tough work, but it is the most important work we do as parents. It requires asking the right questions—questions that get beneath the surface and expose motives. I remember sitting with Juan and another couple during a counseling session as he was helping them work through marital conflict. I was amazed because he guided them simply by asking questions. That was genius! I had to go home and try it on the girls, and I have been using it ever since. Asking heart questions helps your kids (and you!) evaluate their motives.

Asking heart questions is different from giving lectures. Do you remember getting a lecture when you were young? I (Jeanine) do! I remember thinking, *Here we go again!* My dad would tell me what I did wrong, that it was bad, and what would happen next. Of course, I knew what to expect the next time I disobeyed—another lecture. No relationship. No help. Just words. A lecture doesn't count as communication; it's a monologue. Instead, our goal in getting to the heart is to draw out the reasons behind their sin, their motivation, in order to identify the sin underneath the sin. This allows us to get to the root of the problem and not just the fruit. It helps us address the real issue and not just the symptoms. Remember what Jesus said: "For from within, out of people's hearts, come evil thoughts, sexual immoralities, thefts, murders, adulteries, greed, evil actions, deceit, self-indulgence, envy, slander, pride, and foolishness. All these evil things come from within and defile a person" (Mark 7:21–23). That's what we're after—identifying the motivation of the heart that led to the outward disobedience and sin.

Let's think about what getting to the heart looks like. Say two children are fighting over a toy. It's a common occurrence. One child has the toy and has been playing with it, then the other child takes it. Immediately, we have a justice issue. "That's not fair. I had it first!" thinks the first child. "But I want it!" the second child blurts out. How will we handle this situation? Often parents are tempted to address only the justice issue—"Who had it first?" If only it were that simple. The problem is that the heart is not addressed. Ask the "why" question: "Why did you take your brother's toy?" The child may not know at first. So guide your child with more penetrating questions: "Hey, what's going on? Do you know why you snatched the toy out of your brother's hand? What was going through your mind? What were you feeling? Did he make you angry? Did you feel sad that he had that toy and you didn't?"[14] We don't really know why our children disobey until we dig deep enough to learn their heart motivations. And that takes time. It requires patience. It requires you helping them put words to their feelings—"What happened that made you feel upset (or impatient, etc.)?" Then guide them to see if their response to the conflict brought about a blessing or a curse. "Did your sinful response make this better or worse?" It would be easy to just ask what happened, and then discipline your children. But getting them to search their own hearts is vital. By doing so, you are equipping them to discern their own hearts for the rest of their lives.

Repentance

Once you've worked through the heart issues, and there is confession of sin, you want to walk your child through biblical repentance. True repentance reconciles broken relationships. At first, you will need to teach them the words to use. Too often we ask children to say, "I'm sorry," but there is no real contrition. Instead, help them see their need to confess specific sin to the specific person(s) they sinned against. "I'm sorry I snatched the toy from your hand. That was selfish (heart motivation)." Once sin is confessed, teach that forgiveness must be requested. "Will you please forgive me for taking your toy?"

Remember also that modeling confession and repentance for your children will leave a powerful impression. Juan and I worked hard to make our home a safe place to confess sin and where repentance and reconciliation were a natural and normal way of life. We modeled it in our marriage and in our relationships with our girls. I often prayed that God would make our home a confessing home, a place where the gospel was on full display.

Let's wrap this section up with a personal example. One of our girls was struggling in school, and part of it was her own laziness. She didn't want to do the hard work of studying. We homeschooled, so she took all her tests at home. I went to grade her biology test, and when I came to the short answer section, I noticed that her answers had nothing to do with biology. I was perplexed. But as he so often does, the Lord gave me wisdom. So, I went to get the answer key for physical science. Wouldn't you know, she had copied the answers from the answer key, but it was the wrong answer key. I was shocked, but also a little amused. The poor girl didn't even know how to cheat well; I should be thankful. The easy thing would have been to verbally chastise her and ground her. That would satisfy the "she needs to be punished" side of me, but it wouldn't get to her heart. So I called her in for some "heart therapy," and it started with questions.

> "Sweetheart, I am grading your biology test, and I notice that these answers have nothing to do with biology. Do you want to tell me what is going on here?"
>
> Silence.
>
> "I think it will be better if you tell me what happened, instead of me telling you what happened. It's always better to confess your own sin."
>
> She confessed. Then came more questions.
>
> "Why did you feel you needed to cheat?"
>
> "Because I didn't know the answers."
>
> "Why didn't you know the answers?"

See what I was doing? I was guiding her to the conclusion I want her to make without telling her. I knew she didn't want to study. She knew it too, but she needed to verbalize it. Then I kept digging and got to the heart of it. Maybe she didn't understand the concepts and needed help but waited too long. Maybe she has a learning disability and struggles with learning and test taking. There are a myriad of reasons why she may have felt the need to cheat. We should want to help our kids unpack all the muddled thinking that's going on in their minds and hearts. After that discussion, there were consequences. There needed to be consequences. This is gracious parenting with a backbone. And you need a strong backbone in parenting!

Disobedience: Corrective Discipline

I bet you want to know what the consequences were for my cheating daughter. Guess what? It may frustrate you, but I'm not telling you. Why? Because each child is different, and what was right for my daughter in that situation might not be right for yours. Like me, you may want a formula, a set of rules. I love math because 1+1=2 every single time. The formula for the area of a square is the same no matter the size of the square. Amazing! Unfortunately, parenting isn't like that. As much as I would love it, there is no formula for parenting your children. You have to know each child. You have to know what makes that child tick, what motivates the child. For some of our girls, giving them "the look" was enough to stop them in their tracks. That was the kind, tenderhearted, and sensitive child. Then there's the one you could talk to, reason with, and correct, but nothing seemed to work. Still, there must be consequences. God calls us to be faithful parents, no matter how our children may respond to our discipline. So as we consider how to apply corrective discipline in these middle years, we will continue to employ the three levels of discipline we established in chapter seven: exhortation, rebuke, and chastisement. Keep in mind that these three levels work together and are often intertwined. Still, for the sake of discussion, we will treat each one separately.

Exhortation

Remember that an exhortation is a serious, urgent appeal to do something. It is a personal or solemn word of advice or warning. Often, our warning may highlight consequences, both logical and natural, like we discussed in the previous chapter. For example, our girls were not allowed to play until their schoolwork was done. After school, they only had one chore to complete. Once done, they had the freedom to enjoy a snack and play. The girls knew if they failed to complete their schoolwork, they couldn't join us during playtime. That was a logical consequence: the loss of freedom. What do you do if your child doesn't clean up his toys when asked? You confiscate the toys for a week. That's a logical consequence. I cannot tell you how many toys and miscellaneous items lived in our laundry room because they either weren't put up or taken care of. No nagging. No bribing.

No threatening. No repeating. Just exhorting. The expectation was faithful obedience.

As we have seen, natural consequences are often the best teachers. Say your son leaves his basketball outside after you've warned him again and again to put it up when he's done. The natural consequence is that the ball gets ruined in the weather or, worse, stolen. Now, if you immediately go out and buy him a new basketball, you aren't helping him learn the important lesson that he needs to take care of his property.

Often, as our children age, natural consequences will revolve around money. So, if your child is playing ball in the house, after you have told him not to, and the lamp gets knocked over and broken, what would be a natural consequence? He replaces it! He has no money? That's fine. Give him jobs around the house so he may earn the money. Be sure to give him real work. That's what we adults have to do, isn't it? We must teach our children to take responsibility for their actions.

Rebuke

The next level is a rebuke; this comes in the form of verbal correction. And wise children receive rebuke given in love. As Proverbs 9:8 declares, "Don't rebuke a mocker, or he will hate you; rebuke the wise, and he will love you." We must correct in love and not in anger. If you are constantly yelling at your children when you correct and rebuke them, it will be hard for them to be thankful for your correction. Often we yell because we are frustrated with our children's behavior and don't know any other way to correct them. That is not loving correction.

Loving correction is also grounded in God's Word. This is definitely the stage when we are pouring Scripture into our children's minds and into every situation we face together. When we are teaching, training, correcting, and rebuking, we are helping them reorient their thinking to live according to God's ways. We don't just want them to stop fighting with their siblings; we want them to love one another as Christ has loved us (John 13:34). We don't want them to just stop complaining, we want them to have thankful hearts (1 Thessalonians 5:18). Don't just throw the negative passages at them, the ones where they stoned disobedient kids. We can't scare them to Jesus; instead, let's show them the blessings of obedience, the riches we have in Christ!

Chastisement

The last level of discipline is chastisement. This is a special category and is saved for willful rebellion and defiance. This is for the deep foolishness that is bound up in their hearts. In a perfect parenting world, most of the chastisement is administered in the early years up until about age six. Then we pray it is used less and less, because they are less and less defiant. But we don't live in a perfect world, and your children will push the boundaries and see if you really mean business. If you have already laid the framework, they know what will happen when they defy you, and if they have forgotten, they will quickly remember.

Reb Bradley, in his book *Child Training Tips*, offers the categories of active and passive rebellion to help guide us in determining whether a behavior needs chastisement.[15] Active rebellion is the easiest to identify. When children run the other way when we tell them to come sit down, we know that's active rebellion. But how about when your eight-year-old won't take no for an answer and is arguing with you to change your mind? Or perhaps you tell your child to turn off the TV, which he does, but when you walk out of the room, he turns it back on. Those are also instances of active rebellion.

Passive rebellion is where the attitude comes in. They may obey your commands, but they are whining and complaining, rolling their eyes, or stomping their feet. There are so many instances of disobedience that we deal with in this stage, but what might be the most difficult is the sass and bad attitudes. My girls had special muscles around their eyes and were able to roll them in great displeasure when something happened that they didn't like. Then would come the big sigh, the rolling of the eyes, and off they would stomp. I hear so many parents say in frustration, "I just don't know what to do about the attitude!" Let me tell you, friends, you had better deal with that attitude the first time you see it, because it will only grow. And if you're not vigilant, a bad attitude will wreak havoc on the relationships in your home.

The attitude, the back talk, and the rolling of the eyes are all kingdom issues. As Paul Tripp reminds us, we all have our personal kingdoms over which we are the rulers.[16] So long as everyone abides by the laws of our kingdom, all will be well. But the moment someone violates our laws, any of our laws, it's "off with their heads!" Maybe your son is playing outside, and it's time for dinner. You call him inside, but he declares he's not done and will come when he's ready. Or maybe you praise your daughter for a lovely drawing that took significant time to finish. But her sister, who craves attention, becomes jealous and rolls her eyes. That is disobedience and shows a rebellious heart, which cannot be left to itself. We must take the time, at every instance, and remind our children that there is only one King, and his name is Jesus. And in his wisdom, Jesus has placed you, Mom and Dad, as his representative authority in our home. Faithful obedience involves a humble heart, one that is truly submitting to your authority under Christ.

Rebellion, both passive and active, requires correction. Biblical chastisement at this stage looks the same as in the early years, but please make sure that it's complete with restoration of the relationship. Chastisement without repentance and restoration of the relationship is incomplete and will harden your child's heart. And remember: as your child matures, chastisement should be used less and less. Our goal is for our children to take ownership of their own sin and humble themselves under our leadership.

Do Not Provoke Your Children to Anger

Sometimes in our rush to correct our children, we may get it wrong. Wouldn't it be better if we had the information we needed to get it right before we corrected our children? This is where the appeal comes in. An *appeal* is a discussion or question rooted with a humble attitude that provides information we may not have or allows a child to ask for clarification. For example, my daughter might not like a decision I have made for her, but she may humbly accept it with a "Yes, ma'am" and ask for clarification so that she can gain understanding. In some cases, a child can offer us new information as to why obedience is difficult. For example, maybe you, Mom, tell your son to take out the trash. As usual, you expect immediate obedience. However, he might respond with, "Mommy, may I please appeal? Daddy just told me to clean my room before supper." That is important information you didn't know. To obey you in that moment would require him to delay obedience to Dad, which is not acceptable. Clearly, the child is not trying to get out of the task you've given him. He's wrestling with how to fulfill your expectation when he has conflicting directions. Or maybe you asked your daughter to clean up a project she hasn't finished, but she would like to continue it later. A humble appeal would be the perfect way for her to make a request to leave her supplies out for later while still acknowledging and submitting to your authority. The difference between an appeal and a complaint is the heart posture; an appeal arises from a submissive spirit that wants to obey.

Learning to appeal comes with their maturity and your guidance. Teach your children to appeal with a humble heart. It takes training just like every habit we've covered so far. They may try to whine and give you more information or ask for clarification with tears in their eyes. Redirect them and help them appeal appropriately. When they come back to you with self-controlled voices, show them how to request an appeal. "Yes, Mommy. May I please appeal?" Then you can hear what they have to say and make a decision accordingly. The appeal is a tool in your children's toolbox that helps reduce their frustration. Remember that we want to create an environment where it is easy for our children to come to us and share their concerns. And we want to help them obey as best as we can.

Another way to reduce frustration, and, therefore, the need for chastisement, is the five-minute warning. Giving children a short time frame to prepare for a specific task can make the difference between faithful obedience and a defiant meltdown. When your daughter is at a friend's house for a playdate and you arrive to pick her up, instead of immediately demanding that she drops everything and leaves with you right away, say, "All right, sweetheart, you have five minutes left to play. Then we will clean up and go home." This way, you've warned her that the end of playtime is coming, but you've given her the chance to bring that time to a close peacefully. It won't guarantee that your child will be cheerful every time the five minutes expire. You may still need to correct, but it makes obedience easier, and therefore much more likely.

Practical Application: Using Scripture to Address Contentiousness

What about the angry, contentious child? Doesn't every family have one? We did, and at times, they all seemed to be. They would be playing together, and suddenly, there would be an outburst. This is a frequent complaint of parents at this stage: "They just don't get along!" What does the Bible say about that? Quite a lot! Proverbs 20:3 tells us that "honor belongs to the person who ends a dispute, but any fool can get himself into a quarrel." If your children are arguing, pull out this verse and ask, "Are you worthy of honor here, or are you being foolish?" Then you can guide them to the positive trait after you have heard the situation. "The Bible tells us that we should have the fruit of the Spirit." If your child is not a believer, remind her that you are praying that God would give her a new heart and the gift of the Spirit so that he would produce this fruit in her life. Memorize a Scripture song to help them remember these truths! Then ask them, "Are you showing love and peace to each other? Are you both being kind and gentle with one another?" Remind them that Romans 12:18 tells us that we are to work hard at living at peace with one another. And the consequence of arguing with your sister is a loss of freedom. If they are unable to live at peace with one another and be honorable by not starting a fight, then they cannot play together. I would have her sit in the hallway until she was ready to repent, confess, make it right with her sibling, and try again. They might fail, but it would give us another opportunity to talk about Scripture and God's good will for us!

Each moment of disobedience and struggle in your children's lives is a teaching moment, not an inconvenience. It's an opportunity to point them to Christ, who is kind and gracious, who restores us when we confess our sin, when we repent, and when we humble ourselves. We need to ask ourselves, "How can this discipline experience help lead my children closer to Jesus?" We can show them how we want to walk alongside them and help them submit to Christ.

Building a Relationship with Your Child

We'd like to emphasize, once again, the importance of relationships. It's a vital aspect of parenting during this stage. How you relate with your children on a daily basis and at a personal level will give you the credibility with your children to see you through times of correction and discipline. They must know you are for them and never against them. When you have worked hard at positive instruction and training as well as corrective discipline using various levels, this opens the door for healthy relationships.

A key component of relationships during this stage is building a strong family identity. It starts with phrases such as, "We are Sanchezes and Sanchezes don't do that." Your kids will likely grow somewhat discontented with the fact that your family doesn't allow things that other families do. Give them reasons for that and let them know that's not what your family does.

We also worked on building family memories that might be as simple as riding bikes on the weekend, or visiting undiscovered areas around where you live. Have regular family adventures! Setting aside a protected night of the week for family night is also helpful. That was a special night with fun food and an activity which might be as simple as a movie. As the girls grew and started going out with friends, they knew that Friday night was saved for family night.

Another way we worked on building a strong family identity was making sure our girls worked on their sibling relationships. Conflict is a part of family life, but unresolved conflict should not be. We often told them that their siblings were their best friends, and they would always have that relationship if they worked on it. This takes intentional training and applying Scripture as Satan wants to divide our families.

Are you sacrificially taking time for your kids? We are all tired at the end of the day, and we can't wait for the kids to get to bed so we can have a break, but think about how you can build family identity and relationship during those evening hours. Two things that were key for us were reading aloud together as a family and playing games. The girls learned how to win and how to lose, how to be gracious, how to not cheat even when tempted, and how to defer to others. There was always much laughter, and we made many memories around the table playing games. Now, we take games on vacation and even have parties where guests bring their favorite games, and we all take turns playing with different groups.

Paying attention to your kids is a very important part of building relationships. You probably think you pay attention to them because you take them to school and to their sports activities, buy them things they need, and cook them dinner. But do you really pay attention to what they are saying? Or are you looking at your phone while they're talking, assuming you can multitask? Do you know who they are becoming? Do you ask them questions and really listen? Do you try to learn about the things they like and engage when they are telling you about their favorite movie or band? Are you enjoying time together outside the home? Camping while our girls were in this stage was one of the bonding activities we did. Being outdoors without the distraction of devices allowed for many free-flowing conversations. That sacrifice of truly listening and getting to know your child will fill the bucket of relationship that's needed for the next phase of parenting—the teenage years.

Conclusion

My (Juan's) undergraduate degree is in music education. I did my student teaching in an elementary school for the first half, then in a middle school for the last half. That elementary school experience reminded me just how foundational those early years are. The middle school experience, though, left an indelible mark. Those wonderful children from diverse backgrounds act out because they are longing for acceptance and seeking affirmation. These are important years.

May the Lord grant us the wisdom, patience, and grace to see them as God sees them, fearfully and wonderfully made. May we constantly pray for God to give them a new heart and his Spirit. And may we give ourselves to provide the consistency and security they seek by creating a safe and welcoming home where love reigns, affirmation flows freely, it's OK to fail, and correction is for their good and God's glory.

Talking Together

As you can see by now, during each age and stage of life, we're trying to lay a biblical foundation, shepherd our children's hearts, and practice corrective discipline. Those are the three areas we want to consistently practice as faithful parents. In this stage, we introduced the concept of relationships. Relationships are vital to faithful and fruitful parenting. As you talk together, think about your child, or think about each of your children. Let's unpack what we've learned together about the middle years.

1. Are you more encouraged or more discouraged about your approach to biblical instruction in your family? What encourages you? What discourages you? What changes can you make?

2. How are you leading your children in order to "get to their hearts" during the middle years? What practical tips or helpful tools did you pick up in this chapter that you can begin to implement immediately?
3. Evaluate your approach to corrective discipline with your children. What do you need to continue? What do you need to change? What do you need to begin doing?
4. Evaluate the state of your relationship with your children. What are some ways you can strengthen relationships with your children?
5. Make a list of topics you'd like to discuss with your spouse, a friend, or your discussion group after reading this chapter.

Chapter 10

Parenting in the Older Years (13–18 years)

Principle: During the older years, we are equipping our children to walk in wisdom and apply the gospel for themselves.

When we moved to Austin, Texas, in the United States in 2005, we were parenting girls in the younger, middle, and older years. Our oldest was thirteen years old. Our youngest was two and a half. Between them, we had a nine-, an eight-, and a four-year-old. By God's grace, Jeanine and I had worked hard to train our girls in faithful obedience. And thankfully, our girls had responded well. But then something began to change. We noticed that our oldest daughter, who had always been responsible and had kept her room neat, was having trouble cleaning her room. She became more emotional. She was forgetful. Needless to say, we were getting frustrated. We were at a loss because she had never been characterized by irresponsible behavior. One Sunday before our church service, Jeanine and I were talking together, trying to understand how to help our daughter. Did we need to be firmer in our expectations? Did we need to discipline for defiance? We just didn't know. Then one of the members of our church, a mother who was also raising daughters, spoke up and said, "Puberty!" Jeanine and I both looked at her at the same time, and she said it again, "Puberty!" We said, "What?!" And she explained that our daughter was going through puberty. She had happened to overhear our frustrated conversation, and she gently wanted us to know that our frustration was because our daughter's hormones were going crazy. Frankly, we were relieved to hear her counsel.

As our children grow older and mature emotionally, physically, intellectually, and psychologically, each stage brings new challenges and new possibilities. It's true that, starting in the middle years and into the older years, our children's bodies are changing, and their hormones are raging. Still, that's not an excuse for disobedience. Sadly, too many parents dread this stage. Even a well-known Christian psychologist counsels parents to just get through this stage, to survive the teen years. But if you've been faithful to fulfill your role as a parent throughout the previous stages, this is the stage where you begin to enjoy the fruit of your labors. If you remember the rectangle model from chapter 3, at this stage, there should be less parental direction, and your child should be taking more responsibility. The teenage years can be some of the best, most enjoyable years you have with your children. By this stage, you have helped your children understand why they should obey and encouraged them to take ownership of their actions. Now, in the older years, you're more like coaches on the sidelines. You've put in the work. Now, you continue equipping them by helping them apply the gospel to themselves and helping them walk in wisdom.

Maintaining a Biblical Foundation: A Proverbial Model

The best way I know to think about parenting in the older years is to follow Solomon's approach in Proverbs. If our children are to walk on the path of righteousness that leads to life, what they need most is wisdom. Wisdom is a gift from God (Proverbs 2:6). While it includes knowledge, it's much more (1:2–6). Wisdom gives us insight into God's character, purposes, and ways, and having this insight shows us the way of righteousness. Helpfully, the Bible distinguishes between worldly and heavenly wisdom. Worldly wisdom leads one on the path of unrighteousness that ends in destruction and death, while heavenly wisdom leads one on the path of righteousness that leads to blessing and life (Psalm 1). During the early years, we should have invested time in laying the biblical foundation that is able to give our children wisdom for salvation (2 Timothy 3:15). And having laid that foundation, during the older years, we will continually reach back to that deposit and equip our children to heed our instruction that they may walk in wisdom. That's why Solomon wrote Proverbs for his sons—so that the wisdom they gleaned from his instruction would guide them in life (Proverbs 1:8–9). And that's why I suggest we imitate Solomon.

As with the other stages, we continue reading God's Word together as a family. Family discipleship is a practice that should happen continually in our homes, but you will have to assess your schedule and establish the best rhythm that works for your family. We want our children to leave our home thinking there was never a time when we didn't sit down to read the Bible together. So, like Solomon, continue the regular diet of God's Word at home. Remember that there are three components to keeping your family discipleship consistent: time, plan, and place. So find the best time for your family. For us it was breakfast. For you it may be dinner or lunch. Choose a simple plan. For us it was no more than a chapter a day. Your children may enjoy more or require less. Then choose a place. We chose the breakfast table. You may prefer the couch or the children's bedroom. As family discipleship became a habit in our home, the girls knew that at breakfast, we would read the Bible and pray. That was our time, plan, and place. That was family discipleship.

Also, as you live life together, the biblical foundation you have been laying all your children's lives becomes a wellspring you can return to repeatedly to instruct, encourage, exhort, and even rebuke and correct. Again, your job at this stage is to equip your older children to use the Scriptures they know and apply the gospel to life—their life. What we're aiming for in this stage is that they walk in wisdom—knowing that God is good, that what he has revealed is right, and that all he does is for his glory. How does this happen? Well, I've already mentioned regular family discipleship. But there are other equipping opportunities available to us and our children.

Everyday Life

Remember Moses's exhortation to Israel to teach their children God's words at every opportunity (Deuteronomy 6:7). In other words, as you live life with your children, take advantage of the teaching opportunities God gives you. For example, at this age, it may be appropriate to talk about unfolding historical events, both local and global. Help your children understand what is happening around them and how it affects them. Maybe a president or prime minister has become the leader of the country, and Christians are afraid for their religious liberties. Take that opportunity to speak about the sovereignty of God. The Most High God is the ruler over the kingdoms of the world, and he sets up rulers and deposes kings (Daniel 4:17, 25). No matter who the leader of our country is, God is sovereign, and the ruler serves at the pleasure of God. Consequently, Christians are free to submit to them (Romans 13:1) and to serve them (Daniel 1). But Christians do not need to be afraid of them because God will tear down all the human kingdoms and establish his eternal kingdom (Daniel 2:44–45). Almost any daily event is an opportunity to point your children to the glory and wisdom of our God.

Regular Conversations

As we saw in chapter 7, the book of Proverbs points out a number of ways for us to talk with our children. Not only should we have conversations about the blessings of obedience, but we should also warn about the dangers of disobedience. Ask your children about their joys, about what excites them. And when your child is down or discouraged, take notice and initiate conversations. Your life with your older children and adolescents should be marked by regular conversations. They should be happening all the time. Certainly, at this awkward age, many teens don't want to initiate conversations. In fact, even when you try to start conversations, they may shy away from them. Don't allow them to dictate the terms of your relationship. Be gracious, kind, and understanding. Assess when the best time is to talk. But you must engage with them. You must initiate conversations. Take advantage of strategic opportunities to address serious topics. Take puberty, for example, which we'll discuss at greater length below. That stage brings many changes to a child's life. This is an opportunity to have conversations about how God created us as male and female. At some point, it will be appropriate to talk about God's design for marriage and sexual relations within marriage. My point is simply this: look for regular and natural opportunities to have conversations with your children.

There is a myth that it's enough for parents if they spend quality time with their children. I say it's a myth because what people fail to realize is that quality time flows out of quantity time. In other words, it is in spending time together and talking to one another about even little things that we find those meaningful moments that mark us for the rest of our lives. So talk with your children. Cultivate an environment where it is safe to talk about anything! This is key. You want your children, especially during the older years, to feel free to come and speak with you, rather than their peers.

Local Church

During the older years, you are discipling your children not just to love Christ but also to love his bride. Young people commonly come to faith in Christ during these years. It is often the time when children are considering the claims of Christ. Your faith is becoming their faith. As young people wrestle with the truth of the gospel you may experience times of rebellion. Keep in mind that they are rebelling primarily against Christ and his lordship. But when young people embrace the truth and beauty of Christ, then church takes on a new meaning. Your children will gain a greater understanding of the place of the church in God's plan. Now it's not something they go to; it's something they're a part of.

Now, instead of being told to serve others out of duty, they should, as followers of Christ, serve others out of joy. Now, instead of you giving them a few coins to put in the offering plate, they begin to understand the joys of generosity. Your love for the church will impact your children. If you love the church, when your children leave your home, so will they.

Far too often, we think there is a magic formula for parenting. Parents are always looking for it. Let me assure you, this book is not it. We're just fellow travelers on this journey called parenting. And on that journey, we've learned that there is no shortcut to faithful parenting. We're parenting for the long term. We're parenting with eternity in mind. Remember that God's desire is to have children who reflect his image. And he is reproducing these children in Christ, through the preaching of the gospel, by the power of his Spirit. It is at this stage that it becomes most clear that parenting is nothing more than making disciples. Our children are faced with tremendous challenges to living in obedient faith and walking in wisdom. It's our job to equip them for that life.

A Hard Life

Life is hard! And as our children progress through the various stages of life, they will face a variety of fears, doubts, and threats. During this stage, as they compare themselves to peers, movie stars, famous musicians, magazine models, or social media influencers, they will often struggle with their self-image. As they try to fit into their peer group, teens often struggle with peer pressure. As the world, the flesh, and the devil unleash their attacks on our vulnerable children, teens will struggle with sexual temptations such as pornography, self-stimulation, fornication, homosexuality, and gender confusion. In order to cope, they may develop eating disorders or even harm themselves. It's hard being a teenager in today's culture. It's even harder being a young, single adult. When life gets hard for your child, don't be afraid to reach out for help. Talk to your pastor. Take your child to a medical professional who shares your Christian values. Find a biblical counselor. Look for other parents who have already shepherded their child through similar difficulties. We do not have to parent alone.

I'm sure I don't need to list all the pressures our children face during the older years. The point we're making is that parenting is meant to prepare them for it. That's what we've been working toward all their lives—that when they face these pressures, they take the wisdom of God and apply it to specific situations. And as we mentioned in chapter 7, we use various strategies present in Proverbs to encourage and exhort our children to choose the path of wisdom that leads to life, instead of the path of wickedness that leads to death (Proverbs 1:10–19). And, as we mentioned above, we do that through regular, ongoing family discipleship and regular conversations. But when our children fail, when they sin, when they wander—as all of us are prone to do—we must equip them with the gospel so that they know how to apply it for themselves.

One of the most important jobs we have is teaching our children the gospel. We've shared it throughout this book because it's so important. But we should never tire of hearing it or sharing it. As parents, we are God's instruments to shepherd our children's hearts to the Lord. And by this stage, our children should know and understand the gospel. What they need is to know how to apply it to themselves in every situation. We need to help them understand that the gospel demands holiness and that, when we sin, the gospel offers forgiveness. They need to know that no matter how far away they wander from God, they are never too far from his grace. To understand that truth, they need to experience this grace from us. Ask yourself these questions: Do you model the grace of God when your young adults sin? Is your home a safe place to confess sin? Do you welcome them in after they've asked for forgiveness? As they experience the grace of God in you, they will also understand that the forgiveness of sin available to them empowers them to forgive others as they have been forgiven. Through all their highs and lows, we need to equip them in how to understand the gospel and apply it to their lives. The good news of God's salvation and the just punishment of sin in Christ is the only hope we have because, apart from Christ, we would receive God's judgment. It will take our entire lives to learn the vast truths of this glorious, good news. The gospel is not just the power of God for salvation to all who believe, but it is also the power of God for holiness.

Corrective Discipline

Understanding and applying the gospel does not mean we don't expect obedience, and it does not mean we don't discipline for disobedience. Admittedly, discipline is perhaps the greatest challenge during this stage in your child's development. We will still emphasize the standard of faithful obedience. That will never change because it's what God expects of us. We will always clarify expectations. They will always need that. But, when disobedience happens during the older years, we often find ourselves hampered as to how to address it.

Now, before we move on, let us say a word about unbelieving adolescents. Throughout these chapters, we have purposely not assumed that children are believers. These principles will be the same regardless of your child's faith or lack thereof. To be sure, Christian children will respond to you out of a new heart and the power of the Spirit in them. Still, they too will need discipleship and correction. Consequently, our goals do not change based upon the faith or unbelief of our children. Our responsibility remains the same: to shepherd their hearts toward Christ, laying a biblical foundation, exhorting, rebuking, and correcting, that they may walk on the path of righteousness that leads to life. Clearly, though, how we apply Scripture, correct, and appeal to our believing children will be dramatically different. They are, after all, not only our children, but because of their faith, they are also our brothers or sisters in Christ.

But whether your adolescent is a Christian or not, during this stage, disobedience doesn't just manifest itself in rebellious behavior or rejection of authority. Like all sin, it emerges from the heart and may manifest itself in attitudes, grumbling, complaining, and name-calling. You may witness it in words, both spoken and written, and you may witness it in a variety of actions. Regardless, the path of wickedness leads to ruin, destruction, and death. So then, how may we faithfully practice corrective discipline during the older years?

With the exception of chastisement, we will maintain the course for corrective discipline we set in chapter 7. By this stage, you are done with chastisement. It is no longer age appropriate, nor is it effective. With this change of relationship comes a change in corrective discipline. We are warning from Scripture. We are exhorting toward holiness. We are rebuking disobedience. We are correcting and pointing them back on the right path. At a practical level, they are experiencing the natural consequences of their decisions. Take advantage of those situations to continue discipling your young adult. And at a parental level, continue to apply logical consequences to their foolish actions.

Since each child is unique, each instance of disobedience is specific, and each of our contexts is different, you will need to take time to consider the most appropriate course of discipline. Again, there is no magic formula, and there is no universal chart that tells us what to do in each instance. And remember that God has given you everything you need for life and godliness. So with all this in mind, let's now go back and think more carefully about what exhortation and rebuke look like during the older years.

Exhortation

This level of discipline should be a daily, common occurrence. Your regular conversations with your adolescents should give way to the warning we see in Psalms 1. To help your children grow in wisdom and learn to take ownership of their actions, we will follow the model of asking questions instead of giving answers. Again, we want to shepherd their hearts by leading them to think rightly and make wise decisions. For example, we might say, "I see you are fooling with this sin in your life, and it concerns me. What are some reasons this could be a dangerous path? What does God's Word say about that? What are some changes you can make to stay away from this struggle?" Then lovingly and graciously exhort, pointing out the dangers of sin and the blessings of obedience. And perhaps the most encouraging question you can ask at this stage is, "How can I help you?" If they don't know what God's Word has to say about their struggle or sin, go to God's Word together and learn. Remember to look not only at the sin but also at the heart issues behind the sin. And always point out the positive character traits that will help them battle that sin. In this level of correction, you are warning them of impending doom should they choose the path of unrighteous, foolish behavior. I know I have to do this as I guard my own heart. For example, when I'm in traffic, and I get frustrated that drivers are going below the speed limit and slowing me down, it is easy for me to lash out at them—of course, they can't hear me. That's how silly my behavior is. But when I stop and ask myself questions to discern my heart—*Why do I get so angry? Why does it matter if they're going slow? Why am I in such a hurry?*—I realize that the real issue is pride. Yes, I think too highly of myself. *My* time is more important than everyone else's, and they're all in *my* way. Now, I am a Christian. And I am a pastor regularly studying the Scriptures. And I still battle with pride. Imagine how hard it is for our adolescents, both believers and unbelievers.

So, the next time a quarrel breaks out and yelling ensues, slow things down. *De-escalate*! Separate the two parties. And ask lots of questions. Start with general questions like, "What happened?" Then move to heart questions like, "What's really going on with you? Why did you get so upset? Is this really about ____________? Or is there something else going on? How did it make you feel when your brother called you ______________?" And take your time. One of the reasons we don't get to heart issues is because we tend to rush to resolve the conflict.

During this stage, your child begins going through puberty and discovering facts about how his or her own body works. You will need to walk with your children during these biological and physiological changes that can be confusing and even shocking. Also, due to the world's influences, their peers' pressures, and their own sinful desires, young people will face various sexual temptations. Our job is to equip our adolescents with the tools we've already gleaned from Proverbs and the rest of Scripture. Our believing children have at their disposal the shield of faith with which to battle sin and temptation. At this stage, we are appealing to the biblical foundation we have already laid. We are exhorting our adolescents to call upon all the wisdom we have taught them (Proverbs 5:1–2). So the main weapons our children will wield against sexual sin and temptation are the Word of God and faith (for believers), undergirded with prayer (both theirs and ours).

Satan is roaming around like a lion seeking to devour our children (1 Peter 5:8). While they're vulnerable in different ways throughout the various stages of their lives, the stage of adolescence is a particular challenge. They are discovering who they are. They are learning about their sexuality. And they are looking to fit in and be accepted by their peers. This is why it's important they feel accepted at home and are free to be themselves. And for believing children, we must constantly remind them of their standing in Christ. They are accepted before God on the basis of Jesus's life, death, and resurrection, and, as a result, they have a new family. Hopefully, during this stage, you will begin to see the fruit of your biblical instruction and godly example during the earlier years. As parents of adolescents, we must be there every step of the way, no matter what they face, walking with them in love and pointing them to the wisdom of God that they may walk on the path that leads to life.

Rebuke

Sadly, there will be times when, even with all our exhortations, our children will sin. Like us with our heavenly Father, sometimes they will disobey. While chastisement is no longer a viable option, we may still use rebuke with great effect. Remember that a rebuke or reproof is a word of correction when your child has done something wrong. Say your young adult has decided not to heed your warnings, the warnings of Scripture, really, and chooses a foolish path instead. Depending on the sin, natural consequences tend to follow foolishness at this stage—the most obvious is financial: a speeding ticket, replacing property, fines, or debt. For example, if your daughter chooses to drink alcohol and drive, the natural consequence may be an encounter with the police, a trip to the local jail, or even a court date. Added to these is likely a large fine, or, in the worst cases, an accident, or, God forbid, death. Those are all natural consequences. Remember that our rebuke should never be an "I told you so!" With natural consequences, we may not need to say much. We definitely shouldn't lecture. The consequence itself is a sufficient rebuke. Still, you will want to help them process God's justice in allowing a natural consequence to address their sin. And when you must rebuke, don't allow your anger to become sinful against your child who has sinned. Remind yourself of our aim: to lead our children on the path away from ruin, destruction, and death and direct them on the path that leads to joy, blessing, and life.

There will be occasions, though, when an older child sins, and it requires a rebuke, followed by a logical consequence. We want to offer correction. We should offer correction. But we will also want to ask questions to get to the heart. Still, after the rebuke, the questions, and the conversations, we must apply logical consequences. These will require some thinking and creativity on your part, but the consequences must make sense to your young adult. The punishment must fit the crime. With correction at this stage, we are seeking to move our adolescent from our parental direction to taking responsibility for their own actions. But even at this stage, one of the most logical consequences for disobedience is loss of freedom.

At this stage, for example, a particularly important area you'll need to monitor is their smartphone. We forget that a smartphone is a powerful computer that just happens to make phone calls. Because of its power and possibilities, predators lie in wait for your adolescent. But your child doesn't only face predatorial dangers from the World Wide Web. Arguably, the greater danger is simply being lured into being consumed by the ever-inviting screen. Consequently, the phone is a freedom that, if not used correctly, should be taken away. Hear this firm warning: your young adult's phone connects them to competing voices that are calling them to walk down the path that leads to destruction. So think long and hard before giving them this freedom. And do not think twice about taking it away when it is abused. In our house, we consistently sought to monitor our girls' texts and social media platforms. For a season, we read every text. That may sound a little extreme to some, but, I (Juan) reasoned like this: (1) they're my phones since I pay for them, (2) they shouldn't be involved in communication that they would not want us to see, (3) the phone was a tool for us to be able to communicate with them when they weren't with us, and (4) to have a personal phone was a privilege that could be taken away at the first sign of abuse. While our girls may have complained at times that we didn't trust them, we let them know it was our job to protect them from their own poor choices. Then, when they could trust us and showed responsibility in the use of their phones, they also earned greater privileges. That's what we're trying to do at this stage: shepherd them to apply the wisdom of God's Word to all of life in order to walk on the path that leads to life.

Of course, as with all stages, we want to lead our children through the process of confession of sin, repentance, and reconciliation. It is a joy when sinners confess their sins on their own. In order to reconcile relationships that have been affected by a sin, we need to understand what repentance looks like for the specific sin. For example, when tax collectors came to receive John's baptism of repentance, they asked, "Teacher, what should we do?" John told them, "Don't collect any more than what you have been authorized" (Luke 3:12–13). For the tax collectors, repentance meant being just in their collections and not padding their own pockets. Likewise, we have to help our children think through what repentance looks like in each case so that they may reconcile with those they have sinned against. Then, when repentance has occurred, we remind them of God's grace and forgiveness found in the sacrificial death of Christ for repentant sinners. This is how we apply the gospel. We want to make sure our adolescents understand the seriousness of sin, but we also want them to experience the amazing grace of God.

Perhaps because of all the challenges, some parents don't enjoy the older and adolescent years. They are simply trying to survive. We know it's hard. We've walked with five adolescent daughters through highs, lows, doubts, and fears. But these years can also be sweet. Essentially, what we're arguing for is the vital importance of relationship. And this is important because it will be true whether or not your adolescent is a Christian. Even if your children leave your house and enter adulthood as unbelievers, they are still your children, and you still want to have relationships. Perhaps, over time, because you've maintained a good relationship, the Lord will allow you to play a part in their coming to faith in Christ.

The Vital Importance of Relationship

We're not advocating that you become your child's friend. Children need their parents, and you will always be the parent in this relationship, even when they leave home. What we're trying to communicate is that as our children mature, the relationship changes. At first, during the early years, we tell our children to obey "because God has made me your authority." During the middle years, we help them understand why they should obey. But in the older years, we are coaching them to take all we've taught them and obey because they love God and want to walk in wisdom. Think back to the rectangle in chapter 3 that portrays a healthy parent-directed home—strong parental direction in the early years that naturally and progressively gives way to the child taking responsibility as he or she matures. Think of driving a car as an example. It was my (Juan's) job to teach the girls to drive. Before getting a learner's permit, we went to a parking lot in our neighborhood and taught our girls to drive. Keep in mind I had a 1990 Toyota 4-Runner at the time, and it was a manual transmission. Not the easiest way to learn to drive, but our middle daughter picked it up naturally. After getting her learner's permit, she had to drive with someone in the car at all times. Eventually, she obtained her driver's license. Still, we did not just hand over the keys. We still rode with her. We sent her on short errands. I taught her to drive on the interstate. Then, one day, it was time for her maiden voyage alone. Yes, I was nervous! So we prayed! But she drove well, accomplished her task, and came home safely.

In several ways, that is a picture of how parental direction should function. We are strongly directive in the early years, but over time we give more and more responsibility to our children as they are able to handle it. Then, we allow them some opportunities to go for "test drives." And, one day, before you know it, they are driving on their own. That is, you have equipped them to make wise choices, they have proven themselves, and you must entrust them to our heavenly Father who loves them more than we ever could. Unfortunately, when we don't follow this trajectory, we may end up falling into some parenting pitfalls that will frustrate our young adults and harm our relationship with them.

Hands-off parenting

Some parents may be thinking that, since their kids are close to being adults, they should allow their kids to make all their own decisions. They may even be telling you that themselves. This thinking means that your young adult doesn't need your wisdom or direction anymore. This is a dangerous path for all people, but especially for older adolescents. These years are the last you will have in providing any sort of corrective discipline and having daily guidance in their decision-making. Take these opportunities and don't believe the lie that because they are a certain age, they don't need your wisdom. There's no magical age when a young person suddenly becomes wise. For our family, if we are still paying your bills, there will still be some form of authority over the choices you make. And in God's economy, there is still judgment for their sin. They need to learn that in our homes and while under our authority.

Helicopter parenting

Well, technically we may call it *helicopter parenting*, but at this stage, it manifests itself in controlling tendencies. Think of a dad who demands his daughter who is away at college share her location all the time. Or parents who check their college student's phone whenever he is home on vacation from school. Helicopter parenting is rooted in fear. That is a sin we have to address in our own hearts. No matter what we do, we cannot protect our children from every possible danger. We must trust God to protect them, and that trust should lead us to prayer. We found that during this stage, when our girls were away from us, we spent much more time in prayer.

At this stage, we should progressively be giving away more and more parental direction so that our children may take on more and more personal responsibility. We will frustrate our older children if we treat them like five-year-olds or, even, ten-year-olds. At some point we will need to push them out of our nest, so to speak, entrusting them into the hands of our sovereign God. Otherwise, we will create either rebellious children who will flee from our control or overly dependent children who will not know how to cope with the real world. This too is part of our discipleship relationship—equipping them for life outside our home. Don't rescue them—at least not immediately. This is especially hard when you see that either natural or logical consequences to their poor decisions bring them heartache and pain. We should definitely have compassion, but if we continuously rescue our children from their poor choices, we enable them to keep making bad choices and fail to model how the Lord loves us as we see in Hebrews 12:6a, "The Lord disciplines the one he loves."

No place to fail

The lecture, the criticism, the rejection. Sadly, these are ways we manipulate our kids to obey us, or worse yet, to not embarrass us with their poor decisions or sinful actions. Our homes must be safe places for our children to fail, especially during this stage, when much of their learning is through trial and error. They won't always make choices we agree with, and when they come home to tell you the trouble they are in, if you choose the lecture, criticism, and rejection trifecta, they won't come to you with their failure again. You will have proven that you are not safe or helpful. I am not saying we tolerate sin and sweep it under the rug. Sin and disobedience will have consequences. What I am saying is that we should create an environment where our children can come home and confess their sin, where they can tell us they got a speeding ticket, where they can tell us what they did and not hear a lecture, but instead receive God's love. God's love is just and merciful. And we want them to experience it in our home. There have been times when we have asked our kids if there is anything they need to tell us or confess, something they need to get off their chest. It's amazing when your kids trust you with their failures, even though they know there will be consequences, and you are able to lament together, and then help put them back on the right path.

But what if your older children don't love God? What if they're not Christians? The standard does not change. And if you've been faithful throughout your children's lives and you have a good relationship with them, they will be characterized by obedience because they love and trust you. So whether your children are believers or not, we are still pursuing the kind of relationship with them in which they will heed our counsel to walk down the right path. So long as our children are alive, and until Jesus comes back, we will not stop praying for our unbelieving children. In fact, in our faithful parenting, we will model the gospel for them, hoping one day they will embrace it for themselves.

Conclusion: A Bittersweet Send-Off

When our oldest daughter was nineteen years old, she asked us if she could go on a summer mission trip with a university campus organization. We were ecstatic that she was so ministry minded that she wanted to sacrifice her summer to share the gospel with unbelievers. Then, she told us the mission was to California. We live in Texas. That meant we would put her on a plane, and we wouldn't see her for the summer. Well, we agreed to the trip, and helped her raise the funds. When the day finally came, Jeanine and I took her to the airport. We hugged, kissed, and said our good-byes. When we got home, we went into our dining room, looked at each other, and began to cry. It was an odd moment. I never expected that. But for the first time, I realized that all her life, we had been preparing her for this moment. And it hit us. Our baby had grown up. She was mature. She had become responsible for herself. That's why we invested so much in her.

As your children grow older, this discipleship relationship will blossom and mature. You have invested your own life in these children, and one day, when they're gone, they will begin to realize it. They will look back on all those memories. All the read-alouds, all the Bible times at breakfast, and all the times you showed up at their dance recital or baseball game. They'll remember all those times they knocked on your door at night and crawled up in your bed in tears saying it was the worst day ever! They'll remember the time the boyfriend broke up with them, and they cried on your shoulders. They'll remember the investment you made in their education. And you'll remember it too. And you'll thank God for the privilege and joy to have had this stewardship of leading your children to walk in wisdom and apply the gospel to themselves. Then you'll rejoice when they come back and ask for your counsel, when they call on the phone asking for help, when they meet the person they're going to marry, and you walk them through preparing for a wedding, and when you're there for their first child.

Parenting is hard. It's the hardest and most humbling thing I've ever done. Quite often I felt like a failure. But my kids didn't need me to be a perfect dad, and they didn't need Jeanine to be a perfect mom. They need a perfect Savior, and they have that in Jesus. What they needed from us was to be humble, faithful, patient, repentant, and loving. They needed us to picture the gospel for them in every situation. They needed us to be willing to teach them God's Word. They needed us to show them the Father's love. That's all we ever tried to do. And we thank God every day for the privilege.

Talking Together

The adolescent years should be a season of joy as you enjoy the fruits of your labor during the previous seasons of your parenting. Sadly, for some parents, it is a time of grief. Let's talk together and assess where you are and see what you need to do moving forward.

1. Are you enjoying these years with your older child or your adolescent? If not, can you identify what makes it so difficult for you? Is it possible that you were too permissive during the early years and now you find yourself having to give strong parental direction? Try to identify some of the reasons this season of parenting is challenging. Is there a particular parenting pitfall that you identify with?
2. After reading this chapter, what are some steps you can take to encourage your adolescents to pursue God's Word on their own?
3. How has reading this chapter equipped you to apply corrective discipline during the adolescent years? What one practice can you begin applying today?
4. What are some ways that you can begin to strengthen your relationship with your adolescent?
5. Make a list of topics you'd like to discuss with your spouse, your friend, or your discussion group after reading this chapter.

Conclusion

Words of Encouragement

During my early years, I (Juan) went to kindergarten at a Roman Catholic school in Levittown, Puerto Rico. Every morning, a woman came in a station wagon and picked us up for school. One morning, though, my godfather happened to be driving by. Seeing me outside, he stopped. Then, he offered to take me to school. Being five years old, and thinking there was nothing wrong, I said yes. So, rather than riding in a cramped station wagon with other students, I was personally chauffeured to school. From my perspective, everything was fine. But that morning my mother arrived at school with the police because she didn't know where I was. Someone came into the classroom and asked for me by name. When I was escorted outside, there was my mother. She looked distraught. She had been crying. It wasn't the first time I took it upon myself to wander off. I think she wanted to discipline me and hug me all at the same time. That moment is forever etched in my mind.

That incident is but a brief view into my childhood. I was such a challenge that, by the time I was five years old, so I'm told, my mom had to go to a psychiatrist for help. I'm not kidding. When I first took Jeanine home to meet my parents, I was forced to relive all the "Monchito" (my childhood nickname) stories. "Oh, remember the time Monchi climbed on the roof and hid from us while we were frantically looking for him?" "Did you know that when Monchito was about four years old, we were at his grandfather's house, miles away from our house, and Monchi just walked out the backyard. We couldn't find him. We started to panic. We walked all through the neighborhood. Finally, we went to his godmother's house to ask for help, and there he was hiding behind her legs." I'm sure I could write a book called "Monchi's Escapades." Now, why do I tell you this? I share this to end our journey together on a note of encouragement.

I was born in Rio Piedras, Puerto Rico. Jeanine was born in Gainesville, Florida. We had two dramatically different upbringings. I was Roman Catholic. Jeanine was Baptist. We didn't have a lot growing up. Jeanine had a comfortable life. I was the oldest. Jeanine was the youngest. My parents were not believers. Jeanine's mom was a Christian, and they went to church regularly. From the time my family moved to Florida in the United States when I was eight, I attended public schools. Jeanine went to a private Christian academy until high school. Then, she went to a public high school. My parents couldn't afford to send me to college, so I enlisted in the United States Navy. Jeanine went to college right after high school. I came to faith in Christ when I was seventeen years of age. Jeanine professed faith in Christ when she was five or six years old. We were from two different worlds, and yet the Lord saw fit to bring us together. We didn't know anything about having children or raising a family, but the Lord put the right people in our lives at just the right time.

There are three points of encouragement I want to leave you with from our stories. First, your parenting will neither save your children, nor will it condemn them to hell. Let's go ahead and take those two burdens off the table. I didn't grow up in a Christian home, but that didn't condemn me to everlasting judgment. I *did* grow up in a loving home. Both my parents worked to provide for our family. I never resented that. In fact, I was proud of my parents and their hard work ethic. But I was a lot to handle as a child, perhaps too much at times. And yet, my parents loved me. They cared for me. They sacrificed for me. Never once did I doubt their love. And I tested them thoroughly. My parents weren't perfect, but they did the best they could. They didn't practice most of the principles we've shared in this book. But, and this is how I want to encourage you, the Lord saved me through the witness of high school friends. At seventeen years old, I understood the gospel for the first time, and I confessed my sin and trusted in the sacrifice of Christ for my salvation. And since that moment, the Lord has been working in my life to conform me to the image of his Son, that is, to make me one of his godly children. You see, my parents couldn't make me a Christian. Only God can do that through the word of the gospel and by the power of his Spirit. So, Mom and Dad, don't bear the burden of believing that by your parenting you will save your children. Don't think that if you do everything well, your children will turn out right. And don't believe the lie that you've failed or that it's too late. So long as our children have breath and Jesus has not returned, there is time. God's grace is sufficient. He is able to save to the uttermost. Our role as parents is to be humble, faithful, and repentant guides for our children, to establish the foundation of God's Word in their lives, and, as they grow in maturity, to teach them how to walk in wisdom, applying the gospel to themselves. So remember that we guide, we shepherd, but God saves. Only he can make godly children.

Second, your children don't need perfect parents who have it all figured out. They need humble, faithful, and repentant parents who continually point them to Christ. Jeanine grew up in a quasi-Christian home, but her parents didn't apply many of the principles we've outlined in this book either. Her parents sought to be faithful, and they enrolled her and her sisters in a private Christian academy. They took her to a church with a wonderful pastor who faithfully preached the Word. Jeanine enjoyed the activities of a public high school, then life in a sorority in college. Her parents had hoped that she might eventually marry a doctor or an attorney and live the comfortable life that they had. There's nothing wrong with that, but the Lord had so much more for her and for us.

We didn't start out as wise. We had to grow in wisdom through the trials and challenges of life. Since faithful Christian parenting wasn't modeled for us, we had no pattern to follow. We made it up as we went along, following the common sense wisdom of our peers, the world, and ourselves. But God did a work in both our lives, and he opened our eyes to our responsibilities as parents. As we hope you have seen, we didn't write this book because we're parenting experts. We wrote this book because we know what it's like not to have faithful parenting models. We know what it's like to make things up as we go along. Frankly, we wrote this book because we know what it's like to be parenting failures. But we've also experienced the grace of God. We've learned from our mistakes. We've learned from others' mistakes, and we've learned from others' successes. Mostly, though, we've learned from God's Word. Through his Word and by his Spirit, the Lord has changed us. And we've come to realize how important it is to give ourselves to raising children who reflect God's image. Our girls aren't perfect. They'll tell you that. We've faced various crises together. But through it all the Lord has been faithful, and the greatest lesson we've learned is that we're parenting for eternity, not for the moment. Our aim is to present our children complete in Christ on the final day. So, we've learned not to call it quits or throw in the towel in the face of momentary disappointments and temporary crises. Instead, we've learned that God does not waste any of our suffering, not even our parental suffering and disappointments. He is using it all to conform us to the image of his Son (Romans 8:28–29). And whatever hardships we face in this life with our children are light and momentary compared to the eternal weight of glory that awaits us. So, we do not give up (2 Corinthians 4:16–17).

Third, let your home be characterized by joy, encouragement, grace, truth, and, yes, fun! Essentially, we want to encourage you to think about the aroma of your home. If the atmosphere of your home were a candle scent, would it be Joyful or Strife, Safety or Stressful? You will never be able to control the behavior of your children or their attitudes, but you are in charge of yourself and how you respond. Will you allow your home to be characterized by criticism of your spouse and your children, or will you trust the Lord and find joy in the journey? Make family memories together in mundane moments of daily life that will help your home be a pleasing scent to your children and to those who come into your home.

Our final word to you is this: don't let your hearts be troubled. God has given you everything you need to be a faithful parent. He has given you his Son. He has given you his Word. He has given you his Spirit. And he has given you his church—both your local church and the universal church. So "trust in the Lord with all your heart, and do not rely on your own understanding; in all your ways know him, and he will make your paths straight" (Proverbs 3:5–6).

Notes

1. Paul Tripp, *Parenting: 14 Gospel Principles That Can Radically Change Your Family* (Wheaton, IL: Crossway, 2016), 21.

2. Joyce Baldwin, *Haggai, Zechariah, and Malachi: An Introduction and Commentary*, vol. 28, Tyndale Old Testament Commentaries, ed. Donald J. Wiseman (Downers Grove, IL; InterVarsity Press, 1972), 262.

3. Derek Kidner, *Proverbs: An Introduction and Commentary*, vol. 17, Tyndale Old Testament Commentaries (Downers Grove, IL: InterVarsity Press, 1964), 139.

4. Tremper Longman III, *Proverbs*, Baker Commentary on the Old Testament (Grand Rapids, MI: Baker Academic, 2006), 404.

5. John MacArthur, "Ways Parents Provoke," Grace to You, January 30, 2021, https://www.gty.org/library/articles/A325/ways-parents-provoke.

6. I gleaned this insight from an interview with C. J. and Carolyn Mahaney on parenting. See Andy Naselli, "C. J. and Carolyn Mahaney on Parenting," *Andy Naselli—Thoughts on Theology* (blog), February 29, 2008, https://andynaselli.com/c-j-and-carolyn-mahaney-on-parenting.

7. Desiring God, "Prayer is not an intercom to the butler to bring us what we want. It is a wartime walkie-talkie to call down the power of God in the battle for lost souls." Twitter video, November 2, 2018, https://twitter.com/desiringGod/status/1058479614975197184#.

8. While we ground our arguments in this chapter in Proverbs 3, specifically, we are greatly influenced in our application by Paul D. Wegner, "Discipline in the Book of Proverbs: 'To Spank or Not to Spank?,'" *Journal of the Evangelical Theological Society* 48.4 (December 2005), 715–32.

9. I take these principles of corrective discipline from Wegner, "Discipline in the Book of Proverbs," 715–32.

10. Wegner, "Discipline in the Book of Proverbs," 722.

11. Wegner, "Discipline in the Book of Proverbs," 723.

12. "Episodes— Adventures in Odyssey," Adventures in Odyssey, https://www.adventuresinodyssey.com/listen/.

13. Peter Summerlin, "ASLA 2006 Student Awards," American Society of Landscape Architects, https://www.asla.org/awards/2006/studentawards/282.html.

14. I learned great questions to ask from Ginger Plowman's book, *Don't Make Me Count to Three.*

15. Reb Bradley, *Child Training Tips: What I Wish I Had Known When My Children Were Young* (Washington, DC: WND Books, 2014).

16. Paul David Tripp, *Broken-Down House: Living Productively in a World Gone Bad*, Kindle edition (Wapwallopen, PA: Shepherd Press, 2011), location 1970.